CW00517746

Tasting Italy

The Complete Italian Recipes Made Simple

The Classic Mediterranean Diet Cookbook's

Immacolata de Lisio

CONTENTS

INTRODUCTION

What shall we eat?

How many are we at the table?

These are the most frequent questions that each of us asks both in the family environment (*especially if there is the will or the pleasure to change what we eat daily*) and in the workplace (*for those who, for example, have activities related to restaurant or catering*).

The recipe books, in fact, are very useful to satisfy both the taste (*i.e. the goodness of the dishes*) and the view (*i.e. the way they are presented*) and there are really many, indeed too many.

But Nonna Imma's recipe book is unique for two reasons:

- **First**: cooking is a way of taking care of yourself and others; Nonna Imma teaches how to do it with passion and experience.

- **Second**: each of the listed dishes, certainly all typically Italian, has a touch that only Nonna Imma can give.... a little secret, an addition, a surprise that comes from the genius, the imagination and the love that she puts into everything she does.

And here we are in the kitchen....

Nonna Imma has her own way of preparing dishes.

In the book they are divided into topics:

• First dishes

• Second courses of meat and fish

• Side Dishes

• Pizzas

• "Conserve" – for example, fresh tomatoes cooked and closed in vacuum in a jar

• Sweets, creams and biscuits

• Ice cream and "semifreddo" – for example a pudding

• Liqueurs

• And so on

Dinner or lunch or even breakfast are moments of play and hospitality, where food is the element of union: whatever is in the fridge, Nonna Imma is able to combine or rework it quickly, simple and tasty and, in a short time, it becomes a delicious dish.

Every day is therefore a party, an opportunity to lay the table, taking care of every detail, both when the dish is served and while it is cooked.

And it doesn't matter if you are only two to eat or if there is the whole family with friends and relatives and therefore if you become 10 or 20 or even 50 people from 2: **Nonna Imma puts everyone at the table and her book makes anyone able to do the same !!!**

I remember the tables on the beach with pots of first courses, and then the second courses, and then the side dishes, the creams ... not to mention the desserts, the liqueurs and ... in the afternoon, even the pizzas.

And so, in honor of the "*Queen of the Table*", I decided to publish Nonna Imma's recipes, because they are written with love: **Nonna Imma transformed cooking into a art, with which to take care of people.... do it too !!!!**

Enjoy your reading and enjoy your meal.

FIRST DISHES

COURT BOUILLON

Ingredients

1 medium size onion - 1 carrot - 1 celery stick - 1 sprig of parsley - a few laurel leaves - juniper - some peppercorns - sage - rosemary - the juice of half a lemon and its peel - 1 glass of white wine and dry - salt to taste

PREPARATION

In our country we have little use of this vegetable broth that the French call "court bouillon". However, I can tell you that if you use this broth as a base for white fish, the effect will be surprising. Just gather all the ingredients in 2 quart of water and let it boil until the vegetables are cooked, about an hour. Pass the broth and keep it aside in the fridge in a container until ready to use.

GNOCCHETTI ALLA DON RAFFAELE

Ingredients for 5 people

Flour 16 oz - semolina (type of Italian flour) 6 oz - water 20 oz - 3 tablespoons of oil - _fior di latte_ (type of Italian cheese) 6 oz - parmesan 2 oz - fresh tomato sauce

PREPARATION

Preferably in a small dish (copper pan with round walls), boil the water with two tablespoons of oil and salt to taste.

In the water that will have reached a boil, throw the flour and semolina all at once and turn vigorously with a wooden spoon, to obtain a nice ball with a homogeneous mixture.

Let the dough cook over a light flame for about 10 minutes and you will feel it sizzle, at this point you can pour it on the table and, as soon as it has bearable heat in your hands, work it by adding the other spoonful of oil.

The processing must continue for another 15 minutes.

Once the processing is finished you will form sticks of the thickness of the breadsticks from which you will cut many chunks of the thickness of a shelled hazelnut.

Since the pasta does not ready, I recommend, to save time, to obtain the dumplings by forming 4-5 rows of sticks and cut them together.

In plenty of water, put in a capable pot, as soon as it rises to a boil, throw the dumplings in a couple of times and, as soon as they rise to the surface, which will occur after a few minutes, take them out with a skimmer and drain them well.

Put in a terracotta pan a base of sauce or ragù, a layer of gnocchi, parmesan and mozzarella, continue with the overlaps until all the ingredients are used up.

Pass on moderate heat and gently turn a few minutes until the fior di latte begins to spin. Serve, they are delicate and inviting.

Note: if you prepare a greater quantity of pasta; once cooked, the dumplings can be kept in an open container with plastic tissue for 4-5 days; put them in the refrigerator at the bottom and, when serving them, you will pour them for one minute in boiling water, and then season them.

NAPLES-LASAGNA

Ingredients for 8 people

For the pork ragù: pork ham 40 oz - lasagna 20 oz

For the stuffing: sausages 12 oz - ricotta 20 oz - _fior di latte_ (type of Italian cheese) 10 oz - sweet pecorino (type of Italian cheese) 2 oz - parmesan 2 oz

PREPARATION

Prepare a good ragù sauce (see recipe in this book), in the meantime you can proceed with the preparation of the lasagna. Take the sausages and pierce them with a fork, put them in a pan with a half glass of water and let them go on a slow fire so that they soften and have the so-called first cooking (10-15 minutes will suffice). Add a little lard and, by increasing the flame, brown them well from all sides, while at the end you will cook them with a half glass of dry white   wine.
In a capable bowl, dilute the ricotta with ragù, mix well the mixture which must be well blended and homogeneous.

Cut the fior di latte into slices while you can cut the sausages into small touches which, in the meantime, will have cooled. To cook the lasagna it will be advisable to use a large and low pan of 12 inch in diameter which will be filled with water and the right salt but not to the top. When the water boils, add a spoonful of seed oil so as not to allow the lasagna to stick together and throw half of the quantity of these, because they must have the right space to cook evenly. Once cooked, after 6-7 minutes, take out the lasagna and cook the other half. You can now compose your lasagna, taking a rectangular pan measuring 13 x 8 inch. Pour ragù between them, arrange the first row of well-aligned lasagna, spread the ricotta first, pour some more sauce, grated cheese, fior di latte and sausages. Continue the layers until all the ingredients are used up. For the coverage use only plenty of sauce and cheese. Cover the pan with aluminum foil and pass it in the oven for a good half hour at 350° F. In the last 10 minutes remove the aluminum foil to allow the lasagna to consolidate and form a light crust. Let the lasagna rest for half an hour before serving and enjoy your meal. In the old Naples it was used to make this "sweet" lasagna for Carnival and it is perhaps one of the best memories of my childhood; please try it, you will like it! In this case remove the sausages, fior di latte, grated cheeses from the ingredients, increasing the ricotta to 30 oz and adding to this, when diluted in the sauce, a sachet of cinnamon and 2 tablespoons of sugar. You will not be disappointed and, after trying it with your family, you will offer it at a dinner with friends. Good lasagna!

MALTAGLIATI WITH PEPPERS

Ingredients for 6 people

Maltagliati (type of Italian pasta) 20 oz - red peppers 36 oz - onion 7 oz - 2 bags of Chef cream from 14 oz - oil 2,5 oz - butter 3,5 oz - 2 nuts and a half - 1 glass of dry white wine - 1 generous sprig of parsley.

PREPARATION

Toast the peppers, but not too much, on a plate that you will put on the heat over medium heat. Close the peppers in a cellophane bag and let them cool down when closed.

With this system the peppers' skin will come off very easily. Clean the peppers with a damp cloth and cut them into rectangles 1.5nch long and 0.6 inch wide about. In a pan where you put the oil with a clove of garlic to brown, remove the garlic and give it to the peppers, with a chopped parsley, salt and pepper.

Practically, the peppers must remain sustained and calloused. Separately, in another rather large pan, put the finely chopped onion with half a glass of water, to make it soft and transparent.

Add the butter to the onion, and over a low heat, cook a nice blond cream. Complete the sauce by cooking it with half a glass of wine and the nuts. Apart cook in abundant water (5 quart), in the right way, the maltagliati. Heat the onion sauce and stir the cooked maltagliati in the pan, so that they are well flavored and finally add the cream and leave on the heat for a minute.

Arrange the maltagliati on a serving plate and cover them with the heated peppers, put with beautiful grace.

A generous chopped parsley, put on peppers, will complete the dish worthily. It is a very tasty dish that will also go well for an important occasion.

"MEDAGLIONI ALLA SORRENTINA"

Ingredients for 6 people

For the pasta: 3 whole eggs - flour 8 oz - semolina (type of Italian flour) 7 oz

For the filling: milk 30 oz - butter 3 oz + 1.5 oz - flour 7 oz - parmesan 3 oz - 2 egg yolks - cooked ham 4 oz - fior di latte (type of Italian cheese) 8 oz - tomato fillets

PREPARATION

First of all, prepare the pasta by placing the flour on the table and, in the center, the eggs and semolina; start working from the center and mix the semolina with the eggs, then mix the flour until you get a firm dough. I don't put salt in the dough, just salt the cooking water. Now pass the homogeneous cake in the machine, 4-5 times each number up to the number 4 (the pasta should not be very thin) and cut into strips 1.5 inch wide and approximately 11 inch long. Now prepare the largest pan you have, about 12 inch in diameter, and cook the strips in the water, two or three at a time, just a few minutes; then place it gradually on a wet cloth so as to stop cooking. Now pass to prepare the béchamel; melt the butter and pour the flour into it, which you will let toast for a few minutes. A little at a time add the boiling milk and let it absorb; the cream will become consistent and take on a soft and velvety appearance. Add the egg yolks to the béchamel sauce; cool and add the grated Parmesan and finely chopped ham. This is the padding that will be spread on the pasta rectangles with a long blade knife with the foresight to leave the pasta free for about 0.4 inch on all sides. Now wrap the first strip tightly and then another and then a third until you get a roll of about 2.7 inch in diameter.

With the indicated doses 3 rolls should come, place them in the refrigerator for a night, wrapping them first in a plastic tissue paper. The next morning you will find them hard; then take each roll and make many slices of about 0.4 inch.

Take a baking dish, butter it, and arrange these slices on the bottom. You will see how beautiful the dish will look and we can call it "Sorrentine medallions" if on each medallion you will put a slice of fior di latte, a little flake of butter, a tomato fillet, a basil leaf and a pinch of salt. As a final brush stroke, bake at 350° F for about 15 minutes and .... serve. I believe that your loved ones will make you one applause! In addition to having a magnificent appearance and an exquisite taste, you can be sure that this dish is very light for all the genuine ingredients used.

PASTA AL GRATIN

Ingredients for 5 people

Mezzani (type of Italian pasta) 16 oz - butter 3 oz - parmesan 3 oz - fior di latte (type of Italian cheese) 10 oz - 1 glass of milk

Bechamel: milk 1 quart - butter 3 oz –3 tablespoons of flour

PREPARATION

First prepare the béchamel as in the recipe of this book, even if the procedure is the same, the sauce will be less dense due to the lesser amount of flour in the ingredients. Have the grated parmesan and the fior di latte cut into small slices ready; in the meantime, split the pasta into small pieces no longer than 1.2 inch and cook in a large pot, in abundant salted water, for no more than 5 minutes. Drain it and, to stop cooking, lay it on a damp cloth placed on the table.

In a well buttered baking dish, begin to form the layers by putting the pasta first, on which you will pour a ladle of bechamel to spread with a spoon so that it is covered all, a few flakes of butter, 4-5 slices of mozzarella and parmesan.

Continue with the layers until the ingredients are used up. Before baking, pour the glass of milk of the ingredients a little everywhere.

The heat of the oven must be 350° F and, for cooking, it will take about half an hour. For the first quarter of an hour of cooking, it is preferable to cover the baking dish with aluminum foil which you will then remove for the remaining time to obtain a nice crust on the surface.

The dish will be excellent, light, healthy and, the softness of the pasta soaked in the ingredients, will give us a satisfactory result.

PASTA CAMPAGNOLA

Ingredients for 6 people

Mezzani (type of Italian pasta) 20 oz - ripe round tomatoes 40 oz - peeled from 20 oz or fresh tomatoes in equal weight - 1 wine glass of oil (5 oz) - 2 tablespoons of breadcrumbs - grated pecorino cheese 3 oz - 2 cloves of garlic - basil - oregano

PREPARATION

Cook the mezzani, breaking them at about 1.2 inch, for only five minutes and drain them well.

Apart from a salad bowl put the peeled fresh tomatoes; cut the round tomatoes in half and recover some of their pulp which you will add to the other tomato in the salad bowl; then put the mezzani in this sauce, adding half the oil, basil, oregano, chopped garlic and salt to taste.

Now take a pan about 12 inch in diameter and grease it with oil; make a first layer with half of the pasta already seasoned and on this spread part of the pecorino and breadcrumbs, as well as half of the residual oil. Then make another layer are the same system and - on top - arrange the half round tomatoes so as to cover the whole surface. Finally, pour the remaining oil over the tomatoes and salt them. The pan is ready for cooking and you can bake it for 40 minutes at a temperature of 350° F. However, after about half an hour, follow the cooking and - as soon as you see that the tomatoes will appear soft and wilted - it means that the country pasta will be ready.

This dish can be served hot, but it is also excellent cold and can be kept very well. Unlike many other baked pasta, this dish is very light because it is cooked with all the raw ingredients.

PASTA WITH COURGETTES

Ingredients for 8 people

Bucatini pasta 20 oz - smoked bacon 6 oz – ½ cup oil - parmesan 3 oz - sweet pecorino 2 oz - 2 punches of basil - 1 fresh onion - small and tender courgettes 60 oz

PREPARATION

Take the courgettes and, after having washed and dried them well, cut them into small squares; in a rather capable saucepan, soften the well-chopped onion, than put it with the addition of half a glass of water. At this point, add the oil with the bacon, also well chopped, and give the onion a brown color. Add the courgettes with half a glass of water, cover the pan and, over low heat, let the cooking of the latter go. When they appear soft, uncover the pan and brown again. In a saucepan, with plenty of salted water, cook the bucatini which will be broken about 1.6 inch long. Heat the courgettes and their sauce and add the bucatini with the two qualities of cheese, turning over the heat for a few minutes, to give the pasta the chance to flavor well. Finally add half the basil and, from the heat, stir again. Arrange the pasta on an oval dish, sprinkle some cheese on the surface, as well as the remaining basil. The scent of this dish will be inviting and, unlike other pasta with zucchini, it will not be difficult for digestion, as everything will be cooked with a lot of sweetness and that is the main secret to obtain a good cuisine.

"PENNE ALL'ARRABBIATA"

Ingredients for 6 people

Penne (type of Italian pasta) 20 oz – ½ cup oil - 2 cloves of garlic - tomato fillet 20 oz - a lot of hot pepper - basil and parsley

PREPARATION

In a saucepan, brown the two cloves of garlic with the oil, then pour the tomato fillets and cook the sauce for about 15 minutes. Cook the penne, pass the sauce in a crock pot, add the penne and complete the cooking, stirring frequently to prevent the pasta from sticking to the pan. Serve at the table in the same pan with abundant pecorino and chopped basil by hand and finely chopped parsley. It is the typical improvisation dish, made at the last moment, tasty and, strange to say, very digestible.

PENNE CASABLANCA

Ingredients for 6 people

Penne (type of Italian pasta) 20 oz – ½ cup oil - 2 cloves of garlic – tomato sauce 10 oz – pecorino 3 oz - hot pepper to taste – 5 eggs – basil

PREPARATION

Cook the penne, while aside in a pan you will brown the garlic and then add the tomato passed with the chili pepper, cook everything for about 10 minutes. Put this sauce so prepared and from which you will have removed the garlic in an earthenware pan, add the penne that will flavor in this sauce and turn until the pasta has absorbed all the sauce. Separately beat the eggs with the pecorino (half the dose of the ingredients) and, before serving at the table, pour the eggs over the pasta. Garnish the terracotta pan that will be brought to the table with the remaining pecorino and a lot of chopped basil by hand. It is a tasty first course that will be consumed by your diners in a flash.

PEPPERS STUFFED WITH VERMICELLI

Ingredients for 6 people

8 medium-sized peppers - eggplant 40 oz - half-drawn vermicelli 12 oz - cooked ham 2 oz - _provoloncino_ (type of Italian cheese) from Sorrento 4 oz - grated parmesan 3 oz - 1 wine glass of olive oil - ripe tomatoes 12 oz – 2 cloves of garlic - basil - salt to taste

PREPARATION

Take the eggplant which must therefore be medium-sized, narrow and long and peel them with their dark skin; then cut them into chunks and, in a pan with sunflower oil, fry them golden brown. Now take the tomatoes and blanch them to free them from the skin; in a saucepan, where you will have put half the oil of the dose and with a garlic to fry, pour the tomatoes making a nice restricted sauce in which you will flavor the eggplant. Break the 1.2 inch long vermicelli and cook them al dente; after having drained them, mix them with the eggplant adding the parmesan, the provoloncino cut into chunks, the ham into strips and a lot of basil. This is the stuffing for peppers. Take the peppers, wash and dry them and with a small knife make a circular cut on the side of the stem, thus obtaining a small lid that you will set aside. Empty the peppers from the seeds and fill them with the ready-made filling, with the warning to leave some space at the top edge. Take the lids, cover the peppers and lay them lengthwise in a rectangular pan, greased with oil, about 16 inch long

34

and 11 inch wide. Once the peppers are arranged, pour the remaining olive oil over them and sprinkle with salt. Now you can bake the pan for about 45 minutes at a temperature of 350° F; during cooking, you must gently turn the peppers over. When cooked, remove the peppers from the pan and arrange them in a serving tray, being careful to remove the skin from each pepper first which, if the cooking is perfect, will easily come. This dish learn to do it well because in the north, after the vermicelli with clams and pizza, it is considered a typical Neapolitan dish.

TOMATOES STUFFED WITH RICE

Ingredients for 6 people

14 Ripe round tomatoes - 12 tablespoons of rice not filled - 8 tablespoons of oil - garlic - oregano - basil

PREPARATION

Take the tomatoes (about 2.7 inch in diameter) of good quality, pulpy and smooth, not the ones with the groove that are all peel and seeds. With a small knife, remove the upper part from each tomato, obtaining a lid for each tomato, to be kept aside; then, with a teaspoon, remove all the pulp leaving the tomato with the wall of about 0.4 inch. In these emptied tomatoes sprinkle with fine salt and then put them upside down so that the salt drains all the superfluous liquid. In the salad bowl, where you collected the sauce and the pulp of the emptied tomatoes, put the raw rice, 6 spoons of oil, the oregano, the basil, the shredded garlic (2 cloves) and salt to taste. Let the rice steep in this infusion for two and a half hours; you will see that the rice will slowly swell and absorb the liquid. Now take the emptied tomatoes and fill them with the rice leaving a little empty on the rim and cover them with the preserved lids. Arrange the tomatoes in a rectangular baking dish, having first greased it with oil and pouring the remaining oil over the tomatoes with a splash of salt each. You can now put the oven in the oven by adjusting the oven at 350° F for about 45 minutes, until the tomatoes appear soft and wilted. This dish can be eaten hot or even cold for a summer dinner or a picnic.

SIMPLE RISOTTO ALLA FRANCESCA

Ingredients for 6 people

Rice 20 oz - chicken broth (optimum) or meat or nut 1 quart - butter 4 oz - parmesan 3 oz - ½ glass of white wine - 2 fresh onions or ½ onion - ½ sachet of saffron - salt to taste

PREPARATION

Boil the broth and boil, toss the rice, half the butter, the finely sliced spring onions, the white wine. Reduce the heat, because it will be appropriate to use a pan or triple steel bottom or fine pottery that retain heat; let the rice cook without turning it. After 15 minutes of cooking, add the saffron and, after a vigorous turn, turn off the heat, add the other fresh butter, half of the Parmesan and let the risotto rest for another 5 minutes. You will see that the risotto will settle and the excess liquid will be completely absorbed. Put the rice on a serving plate and spread the remaining Parmesan over it. If you want to enrich this risotto you can add a little fresh peas cooked separately in butter, or chicken livers, or sautéed mushrooms and you will have a rich and complete dish. Although the Milanese risotto is famous all over the world and certainly delicious, this one that I proposed to you is just as good, but easier to digest, which should not be overlooked. In fact, in this recipe the rice is not sautéed in butter, as in the Milanese risotto, but boiled. Seeing is believing.

WHEEL OF EGGPLANTS AND CAMPAGNOLA POTATOES

Ingredients for 5 people

Eggplants 50 oz - potatoes 40 oz - ripe tomatoes 50 oz – ½ cup olive oil - 2 tablespoons of lard - 4 tablespoons (3 oz) of sweet pecorino cheese - basil - 2 or 3 cloves of garlic - 1 tablespoon of oregano

PREPARATION

Cut the eggplant, of medium size, in two parts lengthwise, nick them with a small knife for use as a wire rack, sprinkle them with salt and leave the bitter liquid to drain for about 1 hour. After washing them, without drying them, arrange them well aligned in a 11 inch diameter and 3.15 inch high earthenware pan, without missing a few spoonfuls of oil on the bottom. Open half the tomatoes, remove the seeds from them, completely cover the eggplant, salt and add a few spoonfuls of oil, a few lumps of lard, the basil, the pecorino (half the quantity of the ingredients), the shredded garlic and the Origan. On this first layer, lay the potatoes cut into slices that are not too thin, these also well aligned, cover them again with the remaining tomatoes, also open as for the previous layer and complete by salting, putting the remaining seasoning, the pecorino with the smells and finally add a few spoonfuls of water. This dish will be cooked over a very low heat, not failing to cover the pan, for 40 minutes. Complete the cooking, with the pan uncovered, in the oven at 350° F for another 10 minutes. Let it cool down and serve this country dish, very tasty, fragrant and, what is beautiful, easy to digest.

SPAGHETTI WITH BEANS

Ingredients for 5 people

Green beans 20 oz - 2 cloves of garlic - vermicelli (half die) 10 oz - olive oil 3 oz - butter 3 oz - parmesan and pecorino cheese 3 oz - 1 sprig of basil

PREPARATION

Even this dish, very tasty, has the characteristic of having a very delicate and inviting flavor, easy to digest. The execution is quick, just have the beans in the house. Fry the 2 cloves of garlic of a beautiful blond in a pan with oil. Clean the green beans and break them to a length of about 1.2 inch. In a large pot, put a lot of water and a handful of salt, throw the green beans to a boil. After a few minutes, add the broken vermicelli to the length of about 2 inch and cook together. The vermicelli must be not too much cooked, the beans green and soft, but not unmade. Drain the vermicelli well with the green beans and add the oil without the garlic to the other seasonings. Serve on a serving plate. Yummy!

SPAGHETTI DELLA CHECCA

Ingredients for 6 people

Unripe flask tomatoes 24 oz - spaghetti 18 oz – ½ cup olive oil - basil - oregano - 2 cloves of garlic

PREPARATION

Cut the tomatoes into thin slices, put them on the serving plate, round and rather hollow. Season them with oil, salt, basil and oregano. Keep everything in the refrigerator for 2 hours. At the moment cook the broken pasta to a length of 4.8 inch and add it to the plate after passing it under fresh water. For the summer, you will have a very fast but tasty dish.

TAGLIOLINI CHEESE WITH SALMON

Ingredients for 6 people

For the pasta: flour 8 oz - 3 eggs - semolina 4 oz for the sauce: smoked salmon 3 oz - 1 tube of salmon paste – ½ cup olive oil - butter 2 oz - 2 bags of cooking cream - 2 cloves of garlic - 1 glass of Brandy - 1 ladle of hot cooking water - 1 generous sprig of parsley –1 stock cubes

PREPARATION

Prepare the dough by kneading the ingredients and then passing them in the machine several times until you get to turn 4. Cut the dough to size of the _tagliolini_ (type of Italian pasta). In a saucepan, put the oil in which you will brown the 2 well-chopped cloves of garlic, add a finger of water with the broth nut and cook slowly. Complete the cooking with the brandy in order to obtain a blond and restricted sauce. Take a blender and put the salmon already cut into small pieces, the salmon cream and some of the cream of the ingredients, turn to obtain a homogeneous paste. Cook the pasta, heat the Brandy sauce in which you will add the remaining cream, a ladle of the cooking water, as well as the cream obtained from the blender. Arrange the noodles so seasoned on a serving dish and spread the chopped parsley. It is a very tasty first course, very suitable to be served at an important dinner.

TAGLIOLINI STRAW AND HAY

Ingredients for 8 people

For the yellow pasta: flour 10 oz - semolina (type of Italian flour) 4 oz - 3 whole eggs

Green pasta pearl: flour 10 oz - semolina 4 oz - fresh spinach (if desired frozen) 12 oz - 2 whole eggs

For the sauce: fresh shelled peas (frozen if desired) 12 oz - ½ onion - smoked bacon 2 oz - 6 tablespoons of oil - fresh cultivated mushrooms 20 oz - 1 nice sprig of parsley - 2 cloves of garlic

To season the pasta: butter 3 oz - parmesan 2 oz - cooking cream 7 oz

PREPARATION

First prepare the pasta and it will be preferable that you make it yourself, using the special machine. For the yellow pasta, mix the flour, semolina and eggs on the table and knead trying to obtain a hard dough. Pass the pasta for the machine through all the laps reaching the number 5 taking care to go through each number 3-4 times. Cut the pasta into noodles. For the green pasta, combine the flour, semolina, eggs and spinach on the table; if the latter are fresh you will steam them, that is to say without water, instead if frozen you will thaw them in boiling water. In both cases, they will have to be squeezed a lot until they no longer have any drop of liquid and, before adding them to the dough, you will crush them.

For the processing of the pasta, use the same system that you used for the yellow one, making sure that it remains firm (the spinach tends to soften the pasta with the humidity, even if very squeezed).

Separately prepare the peas, finely chop the onion, which you will soften first in a pan with a little water, add the oil and coarsely chopped bacon. When the onion is blond, add the peas to this, if frozen before passed in boiling water, and let them cook gently with the addition of half a glass of hot water.

In another pan, put 4 tablespoons of oil with the garlic and, as soon as it is blond, add the mushrooms cut into thin slices, the parsley well chopped and let them cook gently; generally the mushrooms bring out their water but if needed you can add a half glass of hot water.

Cook the yellow and green _tagliolini_ (type of Italian pasta), drain and season the Parmesan, cream and 2 sauces of peas and mushrooms with the butter. Serve them by placing them on a serving plate.

If time will not allow it, use the already packaged pasta (14 oz per type). But make a little effort to make the pasta yourself and ... what other satisfaction!

STAMP OF MACARONI

Ingredients for 10 people

For the shortcrust pastry: flour 20 oz - suet 6 oz - butter 2 oz - 4 egg yolks - sugar 6 oz - ½ small glass of Cognac - grated ½ lemon - salt - 1 egg red to brown the surface of the timbale

For the stuffing: bechamel with ½ quart of milk - butter 2 oz - flour 3 oz - 1 broth nut - 1 handful of dried mushrooms - sweetbreads 8 oz - chicken livers 10 oz - raw ham 4 oz - parmesan 4 oz - _Mezzanelli_ (type of Italian pasta) 16 oz - salt

PREPARATION

This timbale is excellent, but stick to the ingredients for the padding without variations. The perfect execution will undoubtedly give prestige to your lunch. First, prepare the shortcrust pastry (it will be preferable to prepare it the day before and keep it in the refrigerator until ready for use).

For the filling, prepare a good ragù.

Prepare the béchamel that will be quite firm, spread it on the wet marble table, about 0.4 inch high, and once cooled, cut it into squares. With 1 oz of butter brown the sweetbreads and livers cut into small pieces, cooking them with a few spoonfuls of dry _marsala_ (type of Italian wine) and a little salt.

Prepare the mushrooms: after softening them in hot water, squeeze them and sauté them in a pan with 1 oz of butter, a lot of parsley and a little salt. Grate the cheese, cut the ham into strips.

Now that all the ingredients of the filling are ready, cook the broken mezzanines at about 1.2 inch in length for just 5 minutes. Then let them flavor in a pot of earthenware with ragù and turn until the pasta has absorbed all the sauce.

Take a pan with a diameter of 11 inch and another 3, cover it with a sheet of aluminum buttered on the inside and which comes out a little from the edges; collect the timbale starting with the pasta, the padding, the pasta, again the padding until the ingredients are used up.

The last layer must be only pasta and, on this, add the short pastry that you will have spread on a sheet of oiled and floured paper.

In this way, if you put your arm under the greaseproof paper and turn the pastry shortly, you will see that the pastry will not break.

Remove the superfluous pasta from the edges and with this cut two strips 0.6 inch wide as long as the diameter of the pan, place them on the cross timbale pressing a little, so that the cooking timbale does not rise; finish the edges by closing them with a fork, brush the surface with an egg red and finally prick the surface with a fork. You can bake, the heat of the oven must not exceed 350° F and the cooking must last for at least 45 minutes until the timbale has the crust well cooked and shiny.

Make sure that the timbale is ready at least 1 hour before serving and turn it out, carefully lifting the edges of the aluminum foil and placing it on the serving plate, taking care to eliminate the paper that will come off easily.

Enjoy your meal!

MAIN COURSES OF MEAT

FIORENTINA PORK ARIST

Ingredients for 8 people

Arista (sirloin) 60 oz - 2 cloves of garlic - 1 sprig of rosemary - 1 sprig of sage - black pepper - salt to taste - 3 tablespoons of olive oil

PREPARATION

First, you will need to get a nice piece of pork loin, it is the one from which the ribs are obtained.

Get the whole piece of meat off the bone from the butcher almost completely, even if this must remain partially attached.

Prepare a mixture of garlic, rosemary, sage, pepper and salt and put part of these aromas between the piece of meat and the bones; then make some notches in the meat and, in each hole, introduce the rest of the aromas.

Tie the meat well, put it in a well-prepared pan and let it go to the oven at 350° F for 2 hours (the pork must be cooked well).

In the oven, place a saucepan full of water so that it creates humidity inside. Occasionally, during cooking, sprinkle the meat with the gravy that will form.

Only at the end of cooking increase the oven temperature to 400° F and, for 10 minutes, let the meat brown well from all sides.

As for meat, for me this is one of the tastiest dishes, it is not for nothing that we can say that it is at the top of Tuscan cuisine.

The arista is excellent both cold and hot.

ROAST OF PORK WITH PLUMS

Ingredients for 8 people

Pork ham 40 oz - pitted dried plums 10 oz - 2 glasses of white wine - ½ glass of Brandy - smells (onion, carrot, celery, bay leaf, parsley, a few grains of black pepper, 2 cloves, garlic, marjoram) - 2 tablespoons of olive oil - butter 1 oz

PREPARATION

Two days before packing the dish, infuse the prunes in a light hot tea which will have time to soften.

After 24 hours take the piece of pork and, with a pointed knife, make holes and, in each of these, introduce a plum already pitted and softened.

Tie the meat well and marinate it in a bowl for 24 hours, covering it with white wine and all the smells. In a large pan put the oil with the butter to melt; take the meat, dry it, flour it and brown it until it appears blonde.

Cook first with the brandy then with the white wine that you will have freed from all the vegetables by passing it from a colander.

Add 2 fingers of a glass of water with the remaining pitted prunes, garlic, marjoram and salt to taste.

Cover the pan and cook for an hour and a half.

Discover the pan and keep going for half an hour. When you see that the sauce has shrunk, put the meat aside, pass it through the blender to obtain a thick and homogeneous sauce.

Cut the meat into regular slices, bind them lengthwise, heat them and arrange the slices on the serving dish and cover them with its magnificent sauce in which you can add a bit of mustard.

This dish can also be prepared, and very easily, in the pressure cooker with the difference that the cooking will take about 40 minutes and not an hour and a half. Even in the latter case it will be necessary to restrict the sauce for about 30 minutes.

It is a very tasty dish, very suitable in the winter season, and it can be served with sliced polenta or with sliced potatoes to garnish the dish.

VEAL FILLET STEAKS IN PINK SAUCE

Ingredients for 10 people

Veal fillet 20 oz - mayonnaise with 2 eggs (see recipe or alternatively 16 oz pack) - 3 tablespoons of ketchup - 1 mustard tip - 2 pinches of white pepper - 1 generous sprig of parsley – ¼ cup of olive oil

PREPARATION

Buy the veal fillet already cut into small slices from your trusted shopkeeper, as thin as possible.

At home, beat the slices with the meat mallet giving the blows from the inside to the outside, so that each piece becomes even thinner, I would say almost transparent.

Put the meat in layers in a bowl and, on each layer, arrange the wire oil, salt, pepper and lemon juice.

Let the slices in this sauce for at least 2 hours; due to the presence of lemon the meat will lose its red color and will almost cook.

Drain the slices and arrange them on a large serving dish.

Prepare the mayonnaise with the two eggs, and dilute it again with the lemon juice, add the ketchup and the mustard tip to the sauce.

Finally, cover the meat with this excellent sauce and complete the dish garnishing it with the finely chopped parsley.

In addition to being an impressive dish, your diners will be thrilled. You can also use the already packed mayonnaise by adding lemon juice and other ingredients to it.

CAZZUELA

Ingredients for 8 people

A kale of verse from 40 oz - smoked bacon 4 oz - suet 2 oz – ½ cup olive oil - 1 glass of white wine - 1 onion - 1 bunch of smells - pork stew 20 oz - pork "*tracchiolelle*" (Naples' dialect : it indicate a particular piece of pork 12 oz - 4 chicken legs (to be divided in two) - veal stew 20 oz - 8 sausages - polenta

PREPARATION

Finely chop the onion with the smells and, with a half glass of water, put the vegetables in a well-capable pan, 9.5 inch in diameter and 7.8 inch high, on the fire to soften; add the bacon, the lard and the oil and brown gently until the vegetables have a nice blond color. Add the line, which you will have cut into very thin lists, and let it stun in the sauce, cooking it with the white wine.

Cover the vegetables with 1 quart and a half of water and, as soon as this rises to a boil, reduce the heat and cook for at least 2 hours, until the water has almost completely absorbed.

At this point, put all the meats in the pot, other than the sausages that will be cooked separately, add another half a liter of water and cook for about 2 more hours.

At the end of cooking, the cabbage will appear as a thick cream enriched with all the pieces of meat.

Cook the sausages separately and finally add them to the plate. In a saucepan, put 2 quart of water with the right salt and, when boiling, pour the polenta all at once, which will be turned and cooked for at least 40 minutes.

Pour it into a dome-shaped wet container and leave it to harden, turn it out onto a round wooden cutting board and slice it with a cotton thread.

Serve it with the _cazzuela_ (see the recipe in this book) which will be put in a capable vegetable dish. It is a typical winter dish from Lombardy and you can serve it at a dinner as a single dish.

It may appear a heavy food, difficult to digest but, cooked well with the times indicated, it will be appreciated by all and without this inconvenience.

ROAST OF CALF IN SAUCE

Ingredients for 8 people

Veal walker 40 oz - butter 2 oz – ¼ cup olive oil - a few sprigs of rosemary - 3 cloves of garlic - 1 glass of dry white wine - 1 glass of milk - 3 tablespoons of cooking cream

PREPARATION

Take the baby walker (in Naples the so-called _lacerto_) and tie it tightly by placing the two sprigs of rosemary placed in two gauze bags on the sides before tying it, flour it and pour it into a triple-bottomed pan, where you will have melted the butter with oil.

Brown the piece of meat well on all sides and, when it has taken on a blond color, cook it with the white wine; finally add the milk with the garlic cloves that you will leave encapsulated in their peel.

Cover the pan, cook the meat slowly for about two hours. Monitor the cooking from time to time, turning the piece over.

With the closure of these pans, which are generally hermetic, the liquid should not be reduced; if you see that after the time has passed, the sauce is too slow, with the pan uncovered, let it slightly shrink.

Let the meat cool down to be able to cut it into thin slices more easily; put these slices well arranged in an oval baking dish and cover them with their sauce from which you will have removed the garlic not before having passed it from the blender with the addition of cream.

Before serving this excellent dish, put the dish in the oven at 350° F for 10 minutes and serve.

The meat will be very tender and of excellent flavor.

As a side dish, you can serve sautéed mushrooms, peas cooked in Tuscan use, spinach with butter, of your choice.

QUICK GALANTINE

Ingredients for 12 people

Ground veal 8 oz - minced lean pork 8 oz - turkey and chicken breasts 10 oz - raw ham 4 oz - white lard 3 oz - pistachios ½ oz - 4 whole eggs - parmesan 3 oz

For the garnish: 2 boiled eggs - 1 bundle of lettuce

PREPARATION

In a salad bowl put the two finely chopped meats to which you will add the whole eggs with salt and cheese and work vigorously until you have obtained a nice homogeneous mixture.

Separately, with a little butter, cook and brown over low heat, the chicken and turkey breasts and, after cooling them, cut them into chunks.

Cut the lard into pieces and give it a sear in boiling water, once drained it must be degreased and very white.

The pistachios will be cleaned from their skins by giving them a stamp in salt water (salt water is used so that the pistachios do not lose the green color and can stand out in the galantine).

Cut the salted tongue and the ham into thin strips. After this preparation mix all the ingredients with the meat mixture. To give the shape to the galatina you can take an empty can of seed oil, remove the lid with the can opener and, without washing it, put the dough in it, taking care, every now and then, to beat the can on the table to remove the empty air.

Once the can is filled, close the top with aluminum foil.

Fill a pot capable of water, in this put the can wrapped in various tea towels so that it does not turn upside down during cooking.

Bring to the boil and let the galantine boil for about an hour.

With the amount of ingredients inserted in the dough, the can should not be filled so that with cooking the dough will swell reaching the top of the container.

Once cooked, take out the can and let it cool; turn out the galatina that will come out easily in one block, put it on a cutting board and cover it with a tablet on which you will put a weight.

This is to ensure that the galatina consolidates well by cooling and is well pressed. It will be appropriate to prepare this dish a few days before, so you can put the galatina wrapped in aluminum foil in the fridge.

Remove the galatina from the fridge a few hours before use, cut it into 0.4 inch thick slices and you will see splendid variegated slices for the various ingredients that are in it. Cover the galantine with the jelly (a couple of cans will suffice and you will follow the instructions), put the dish in the refrigerator and, before serving, garnish the edges of the dish with lettuce leaves and boiled egg segments.

It is a dish that will always show off at the New Year's Eve dinner or during the Christmas holidays.

GENOVESE

Ingredients for 8 people

Pigeon or muscle 40 oz - onions 24 oz - 1 bunch of smells – ½ cup olive oil - ham lard 4 oz –1 glass of dry white wine - 2 teaspoons of tomato paste

PREPARATION

After the ragù, which is the Neapolitan sauce par excellence, let's focus on the Genovese which, if done to perfection, will be very tasty.

Take the sliced onions and with the other smells put them covered with water on the fire in a large pan, preferably terracotta and let all the water absorb.

When the smells have softened pass them for the sieve and put this cream in the pan with the addition of oil, ham lard (well chopped) and meat.

With much patience, brown the meat until it is a nice brown color, while the onions have browned.

This can be easily achieved by putting a little water every now and then by scratching the sauce pan.

At this point, cook the meat with the white wine while, lastly, always pulling the sauce, adding the tomato preserve (2 teaspoons).

Cover the meat with hot water (the water on the meats should always be added hot) – you need 2 and a half glasses, also with the addition of a broth nut and cook slowly until the sauce has taken on a good appearance consistent (about 2 hours and 30 minutes of cooking).

With the sauce you will season the pasta, or _mezzani_ (type of Italian pasta) or linguini, while the meat and a little gravy kept aside will be an excellent dish accompanied by a mashed potato or buttered vegetables (such as green beans and spinach).

Note: it is important to use the fat of raw ham as it depends on this the good and tasty taste of the Genoese.

MILK OF BUTTERFLY
(called Milleccio)

Ingredients for 6 people

Maize _farenella_ (Naples' word to say... flour) 20 oz - Lard 4 oz - greaves 8 oz - pork brains 12 oz - water 1.5 quart

PREPARATION

Put the salted water in a saucepan to the right point and, as soon as it boils, throw the farenella all at once (it is practically a thin-grained polenta and light yellow in color).

Turn it vigorously and cook for 45 minutes, stirring constantly.

At the end of cooking, add the suet as well as the sauce obtained by cooking the brains. In a saucepan with a diameter of 11 inch and a height of 2 which you will have greased with a little lard, place half of the polenta still hot, which you will flatten with your hands moistened.

Put the stuffing on this half (the greaves cut into chunks), cover with the other polenta and flatten again with your hands.

On the surface of the Milleccio place a few flakes of suet and bake at 350° F. The cooking will continue for 45 minutes until it has a nice golden crust. It is a typical Carnival dish, perhaps little used today, but very tasty and everyone will like it.

CHICKEN WITH LEMON

Ingredients for 5 people

Free-range chicken 60 oz - juice of 3 lemons - salt and pepper to taste

PREPARATION

Cut the chicken into regular pieces and put them in a large earthenware pan with a diameter of about 12 inch, salt and pepper and add the juice of 3 lemons.

Cover the pan with aluminum foil and put in the oven at a temperature of 400° F. Leave to cook for about an hour, uncover the pan and let it cook for half an hour always in the oven.

Remove the pieces of chicken at this point and cook the sauce over low heat until it has a nice hazelnut color. With a drop of hot water, remove the stick from the pan and stir again, having at this point added the pieces of chicken.

It is an exquisite dish in its flavor that will be accompanied with a mashed potato.

FRIED CHICKEN

Ingredients for 6 people

Chicken of 48 oz - 2 whole eggs - flour 4 oz - salt and pepper to taste - grated parmesan 2 oz

PREPARATION

Take the chicken and, after having cleaned it well, cut it into small pieces, immerse it only in boiling water, take it out and dry it well.

Beat the eggs with the salt, pepper, parmesan and in these introduce the floured pieces of chicken which will macerate in this sauce for at least 2 hours.

In a pan with abundant and hot oil, but not very hot, pour 6-7 pieces of chicken; cook them first on one side then on the other for 15-20 minutes, for the first 6-7 minutes with the pan covered, for the rest with the pan uncovered.

Place the crispy chicken pieces on absorbent paper and, when you have completed cooking, arrange them on a serving plate with lemon wedges.

BOILED MEATBALLS

Ingredients for 6 people

Minced meat 1st cut 20 oz - 4 whole eggs - 3 tablespoons of grated Parmesan - stale breadcrumbs 6 oz - cooked ham 2 oz - step 2 oz - ½ glass of white wine - 1 stock nut

PREPARATION

In a salad bowl, put the minced meat, the crumbled and squeezed breadcrumbs, the eggs, the Parmesan cheese, the chopped parsley and salt to taste; work the dough vigorously until the meat has absorbed the eggs.

At this point, put the finely chopped cooked ham and prepare the crushed and slightly oval meatballs. In a pan with a diameter of about 11 inch, possibly the one they do not stick, you will put a good glass of water with the step and the nut; as soon as it boils, gently put the meatballs next to each other adding the white wine.

You will cook the meatballs on a low heat, taking care to turn them over after 10 minutes of cooking and cook them for another 10 minutes.

You will see that slowly the liquid will have shrunk while the meatballs will have swelled a bit due to the presence of eggs and Parmesan.

You can bring them to the table covered with their good sauce and accompanied by a side dish of spinach with butter.

If the dish is successful, the meatballs, although soft, will not be undone. This is a dish that is also good for those with diet problems.

CACIO AND EGG MEATBALLS

Ingredients for 6 people

Stale bread 8 oz - 6 eggs - parmesan and sweet pecorino cheese 5 oz - pine nuts 2 oz (optional) - parsley - salt and pepper - fresh tomato sauce with 20 oz of tomatoes

I advise you to keep in evidence the packaging of these meatballs which are really appetizing. They belong to an ancient Neapolitan recipe, little used today, no one knows why. Finally, as an alternative to meat, these meatballs are an excellent second dish rich in nutrients.

PREPARATION

Put the stale bread in the water until it has completely softened.

The bread must be a few days before, stale, but not hard and old.

Squeeze the sponged bread first with your hands then squeeze it still tightly with a cloth so that the excess water goes away; it must be damp, logically, but very compact.

In a bowl beat the eggs with the parsley, cheese, salt and pepper, and finally add the bread that you will mix well with the mixture, working it for about 3 minutes with your hands. Let the mixture rest for about half an hour, add the pine nuts (this ingredient is optional) and form some nice medium-sized meatballs, just over a walnut. In abundant oil fry the meatballs, even 5-6 at a time, taking care not to have a strong fire, to allow them to cook even on the inside.

The meatballs must be blonde, crunchy, and the internal dough must have some small holes; in this way you will have confirmation of the good cooking of the dough (the meatballs during frying will have to slightly increase in volume).

Arrange the meatballs on a serving dish and cover them with the fresh tomato sauce you have prepared previously and ... serve on the table.

MARSALA MEATBALL WITH RICOTTA

Ingredients for 8 people

minced meat 20 oz - ricotta 6 oz - 3 tablespoons of grated Parmesan cheese - 2 whole eggs - salt and pepper to taste - 1 glass of dry _marsala_ (type of Italian wine) - butter 3 oz – ¼ cup of olive oil

PREPARATION

Combine the meat with the ricotta in a salad bowl, which must be hard pasta (Roman), the two eggs, the Parmesan cheese, the salt and the pepper.

Do a first energetic processing giving the dough a homogeneous appearance; it will be appropriate to complete the processing by passing the mixture for the chopper.

Form a meatloaf by depositing the meat on a wet and wrung out cloth, in order to have the task easier.

Flour the meatloaf and place it in an unassailable 10 inch diameter pan, where you will have melted the butter and oil, and turn it gently but continuously; roll it up a little.

In another pan, always with an unassailable base and the same size, pass the meatloaf and pour over part of that seasoning where it has been browned, adding a glass of marsala.

Put the pan in the oven at a temperature of 350° F; let the meatloaf complete the cooking, stirring occasionally, for 45 minutes.

Finally you will see that the marsala has evaporated and a magnificent sauce has come out.

Cut the meatloaf into slices and serve it with a mashed potato.

It is a dish with a very delicate flavor that you can also offer in a lunch of a certain importance.

RAGU'

Ingredients for 8 people

40 oz of pigeon or pork ham (in Carnival) - lard 4 oz – ½ cup olive oil - onions 20 oz - 2 tablespoons of tomato paste or preserve - 1 bottle of 1 quart of tomato

IMPORTANT!!!!!

How can we not speak of the famous ragù, a Neapolitan dish par excellence, which has also become part of literature, after being the main protagonist of the famous comedy of "**EDUARDO DE FILIPPO**" on Saturday, Sunday and Monday?

Unfortunately, the ragù of our days will never be what it once was for two reasons:

- the first because the sun dried tomato preserve that was used for this magnificent dish, almost no longer packs

- the second because today's meats that come when matured with systems that are better not to mention, they do not give way to this delicious dish to express itself in the right way

Why was the ragù born in Naples? The beasts of the past raised by us only ate grass and products from our land: the meats were hard, but so tasty and, after the famous 8 hours of cooking, what could our palate taste!

Now other than 8 hours, about 2 hours will be more than enough.

PREPARATION

Finely chop the onions and with the meat and a glass of water put them to cook gently in a capable pan, including earthenware.

As soon as the water has evaporated and the onions softened, add the seasoning and sauté everything on a low heat, adding a little water every now and then to detach the stick formed on the bottom of the pan.

After you brown the meat and onions well, cook them with a good glass of red wine, also put it little by little.

Finally, brown the meat by adding the tomato paste or tomato paste diluted in half a glass of water to it, while finally adding the tomato from the bottle at once. Cook the sauce gently, it just has to quiver; so in 2 hours the meat and meat sauce will be ready.

For the ragù the ziti are used as pasta, while the meat, which will serve as a dish, will be accompanied by French fries, pan-fried peppers and mushroom eggplant. Let's face it!

This sauce when it appears on the table will still give a lot of warmth to our family. But ... Pack it well!

ROAST BEEF

Ingredients for 8 people

Calfskin or buttock tip 48 oz – ½ cup olive oil - sage, rosemary, pepper, salt - 2 cloves of garlic

PREPARATION

With a well-sharpened knife tip, make some cuts to the meat and in each hole introduce a piece of garlic with sage, rosemary, salt and pepper.

The holes in the piece of meat should be at least 7-8.

Tie the meat tightly after having it stuck, as the Tuscans say, with garlic and herbs. In a 11 inch diameter pan where you have scattered part of the oil, lay the meat, sprinkle it with salt, pepper and the remaining oil.

Put it in the oven at 375° F without neglecting to put a pot of boiling water next to it; cook for 40 minutes taking care, halfway through cooking, to turn the piece of meat over and decrease the oven temperature a little.

The 40 minutes of cooking will be enough for you to have the piece of meat cooked to perfection, so you will have the satisfaction, once the meat has cooled, of having magnificent slices of a beautiful pink color that you will cut thinly.

The meat will not be heated, apart from serving its delicious sauce heated in a gravy boat.

What could be better than a nice slice of roast beef? This dish could be counted among the international dishes but, for its success, do not neglect to put, during cooking, the pot of hot water that will give the right humidity in the oven and the meat will be well browned on the outside and very soft inside of.

STEW WITH BAROLO

Ingredients for 8-10 people

Lacerto (type of Italian meat) or walker 48 oz - _barolo_ (type of Italian wine) 1 quart - celery - carrot - onion - 1 sprig of sage - 2 cloves - ½ glass of olive oil wine - butter 3 oz - 1 handful of dried mushrooms

PREPARATION

It is an excellent dish that must be prepared in the winter season and with a pressure cooker, an advantage that is not indifferent to the time savings you will receive, also for the excellent flavor that the meat will acquire with this process. In a salad bowl put the meat, well tied, with a large sliced onion, the smells (celery, carrot and sage), the cloves and cover it with the liter of Barolo or another good quality red wine.

Leave the meat to infuse for 12 hours out of the refrigerator at room temperature, to allow it to mature and mature better.

In a pressure cooker put the toppings and, as soon as they will be warm, with a medium heat, recline the meat that will have removed from its marinade, dried and floured.

Turn the meat on all sides and make this cream of a blond color on all sides. Now add the meat all the marinade with dried mushrooms you have separately made to recover a bit 'hot.

Bring to a boil, close the pot with its lid and, when you see that the pressure has risen to the maximum, decrease the flame to the minimum and let it cook for 40 minutes.

After that time you can open the pan and find that the meat will be soft and cooked. If the sauce is not restricted, roll up the meat and let it shrink a little but not too much, finally passing it through the blender to obtain a sauce of a nice brown color, homogeneous and fragrant.

Cut the meat into regular slices and all together and tightly put them to heat in the sauce; arrange the meat on the serving plate and sprinkle the magnificent sauce on it.

This dish is prepared in Northern Italy, and why not try it too?

It is worth it for its flavor and for the speed with which it is prepared.

MEAT CAKE

Ingredients for 6 people

Minced meat 1st cut 20 oz - 2 whole eggs - 3 tablespoons of grated Parmesan - parsley - oregano - salt to taste - 6 ripe tomatoes (in winter you can use peeled tomatoes)

PREPARATION

Put the meat with the eggs, the parmesan, the parsley and the salt in a bowl and knead the dough until the meat has absorbed the eggs.

Take a low baking pan with a diameter of 10 inch, grease it with oil and spread the dough on it making a disk about a finger thick; garnish the tartlet with the sliced tomatoes, a little shredded garlic, parsley, oregano and a few flakes of steps.

Bake at 350° F for 15 minutes and the pie will be ready.

Serve with a fresh side salad; it will be a new, simple and very tasty dish.

VITEL TONNE'

Ingredients for 15 people

Veal *lacerto* (type of Italian meat) 48 oz - laurel - 1 sprig of celery - 1 sprig of parsley - ½ onion - 1 sprig of marjoram - a few grains of pepper - 1 clove of garlic - a few cloves - water for the broth 2,5 quart - salt to taste

For the sauce: 2 whole eggs - 2 glasses of sunflower or peanut oil - tuna 8 oz - 3 salted anchovies - capers 1 oz - 3 lemons - salt to taste

PREPARATION

Put the water of the ingredients with all the smells on the fire in a capable pot; as soon as this is boiling, introduce the well-tied piece of meat (to make a good broth, the meat must be cold in the water while to make a good boiled meat, the meat must be boiled in the water).

Cook the veal for about an hour and a half, always adjusting with the test of the fork which, introduced into this, will confirm the softness of the meat.

The important thing is that the piece of meat is not unmade.

For the sauce, prepare the mayonnaise according to the recipe. In the chopper or blender, reduce the tuna, which you have drained from the oil, into a thick and homogeneous mush.

The same treatment must be done for anchovies that you have previously barbed and washed.

Add these 2 creams to the mayonnaise, turn until the mixture is homogeneous and dilute this sauce with the sauce of the two remaining lemons (the sauce must be fluid).

The meat, completely cooled, must be cut very thin, this is the secret of the success of the dish, if you do not have the cutter, contact your trusted delicatessen seller.

Arrange the slices on a large plate and cover them with the sauce; garnish with capers and a few sprigs of parsley put with a nice thank you and serve.

What could be tastier and tastier than a VITEL TONNE ' at a dinner party?

Note: at the limit you can also use packaged mayonnaise to which you will add all the ingredients (tuna, anchovies and lemon juice), but it will not be the same and you will not have the satisfaction that you would have if the dish is packaged ALL BY YOU.

SECOND DISHES

OF FISH

CODFISH AT FIORENTINA

Ingredients for 4 people

cod 40 oz - peeled or fresh tomatoes 20 oz – ½ cup olive oil - flour 4 oz - 3 cloves of garlic - abundant parsley.

PREPARATION

This dish is very simple and if you follow the procedure carefully the result will be excellent.

Take some good cod that you will cut into fairly equal pieces, wash and dry them well with a cloth.

Flour the pieces and put them in a pan with the oil in which you have rolled the garlic cloves into small pieces; it will be good to fry three or four pieces at a time making it make a nice crust on both sides.

In a baking dish, place the cod covered with the tomato sauce, a spoonful of oil and plenty of parsley and complete the cooking in the oven for 15 minutes.

The dish is ready to be served. You will eat something excellent and very ... "Tuscan".

PADDED SQUID

Ingredients for 6 people

6 squid (total weight 40 oz) - tomatoes 30 oz - 4 tablespoons of parmesan cheese (3 oz) - 3 cloves of garlic - 1 large handful of breadcrumbs - ½ cup olive oil - 1 abundant sprig of parsley

PREPARATION

The squid to which you will detach the tentacles is well cleaned, leaving only the bag body.

Aside, finely chop the parsley with the garlic; in a bowl beat the eggs, add the breadcrumbs soaked in milk and then squeezed, the parmesan, the minced garlic and parsley, the salt and pepper.

Put the mixture in a pan and on the fire give a very fast turn, enough to barely thicken the eggs.

Fill the squid three quarters with the mixture and sew the top of each with white cotton.

The squid should not be completely filled otherwise, when cooked, the filling would come out.

Take a pan, put the oil in it and, as soon as it is hot, lay the squid with the tentacles.

Brown them for about 15 minutes on both sides.

Add the tomatoes passed with a chopped garlic clove still in the parsley and let cook gently for an hour until the squid is soft.

Remove the seam from the squid, cut them into rounds, cover them with a little of their sauce and serve them with a fresh salad.

With the remaining sauce you can season the spaghetti and have a full lunch.

Note: to obtain that the squid is soft, during the cooking add a bottle cork which then, logically, you will remove. The success of the dish is excellent even if you will use frozen squid and, unlike other frozen fish, just cook them under running water for half an hour before cooking.

SNAPPER IN MAYONNAISE SAUCE

Ingredients for 6 people

headless snapper 32 oz - one egg mayonnaise

PREPARATION

For the times that go by we take a frozen snapper of those without a head but thaw it in the right way: here is the secret why the fish summarizes its fragrance, its softness and returns to being what it was at the time of its freezing.

We remove the fish from the freezer the evening before use, put it in the fridge at the bottom and leave it all night, so that it thaws slowly.

In the morning we take the fish and in the sink, with a stream of water flowing over it, we make sure that it softens completely (just an hour or so).

After cleaning the snapper, put it on the fire in a suitable pan (better the fishpond) and covered with a cold court bouillon; let it boil slowly and with slow cooking (about twenty minutes).

Let's leave it in its broth, with the pan covered, wait for the fish to cool completely.

All that remains is to clean it and obtain all the fillets that will appear slightly pink and soft. Garnish the dish with plenty of chopped parsley, a splash of lemon on the fish, covering the whole dish with mayonnaise.

As a side dish, boiled potatoes, medium and whole, also covered with plenty of chopped parsley with small pieces of garlic and ... enjoy your meal.

SIDE DISHES

MUSHROOMS

Ingredients

Cultivated mushrooms 30 oz – ½ cup olive oil - 2 cloves of garlic - 1 bag of cooking cream - the juice of 1 lemon - 1 sprig of chopped parsley

PREPARATION

Remove the stem from each chapel from each mushroom; with a sharp knife cut the stem; the chapel you will remove the skin and the dark that is in the inside of each of these.

If the mushrooms are fresh, there will be very little of this dark. Wash the mushrooms abundantly, cut them into slices and put them in the pan, where you first browned the blond garlic in the oil.

Cook them first in a covered pan then in an uncovered pan for a good half hour. Finally add the cream, lemon and well-chopped parsley.

With this system you will have an excellent side dish, which is well suited to all types of meat.

ROAST POTATOES

Ingredients for 8 people

Potatoes 80 oz - corn or sunflower oil ½ cup - 1 sprig of sage - 1 tablespoon of rosemary - salt and pepper

PREPARATION

It will be preferable that the potatoes are of yellow paste, peel them and cut them into touches as big as a walnut.

In a pan with a diameter of 12 inch initially put the oil to heat, lay the potatoes at this point which will have to be next to each other, not overlapping, add sage, rosemary, salt and pepper.

Put the pan in the oven at 350° F and cook the potatoes for 20 minutes without touching them.

After this time, take them out of the oven and, very gently, using a spoon and fork, turn the potatoes over, taking care not to break them.

Leave in the oven for another 20 minutes until the potatoes are browned and crispy.

Remove them from the pan and serve them.

Prepare this side dish just 40 minutes before going to the table, since, if served lukewarm, they will not have the desired fragrance and will no longer be soft on the inside and crunchy on the outside.

MASHED POTATOES

Ingredients

Potatoes 20 oz - butter 2 oz - 1 glass of milk

PREPARATION

Cook the potatoes with their peel and, as soon as the pan is boiling, uncover it and simmer on a low heat. In this way, the potatoes will not break and remain intact.

As soon as they are cooked, peel these potatoes and boil them in a saucepan making them fall into a bowl.

Add the boiling milk with the butter, salt and, with a fork, beat the dough vigorously.

You will see that the puree will become light and frothy with this treatment.

Serve immediately.

Even if it is a banal, but very good side dish, this is the system for success to be satisfactory.

The important thing is that the potato is not stored.

PIZZA

PADDED BRIOCHE

Ingredients for 8 people

For the pasta: flour 20 oz - butter 6 oz - 5 eggs - 3 tablespoons of parmesan - 1 stick of yeast (1 oz)

For the stuffing: fresh peas 20 oz - bacon 2 oz - 2 tablespoons of oil - raw ham 4 oz - _scamorza_ (special Italian cheese) 4 oz - ¼ milk - butter 1 oz

For the bechamel: flour 2 oz

PREPARATION

First prepare the bechamel (see various recipes) and separately prepare the peas that will be cooked are half a spring onion rolled slightly in oil (2 tablespoons) and chopped bacon.

For the brioche, dissolve the yeast in half a cup of lukewarm milk and add it to the flour, the beaten eggs to the crepes, the grated Parmesan and the butter cut into small pieces; add the salt to taste and a pinch of sugar.

If the dough, which should have the consistency of a thick cream, should not be very fluid, add a little more warm milk beat it vigorously for a good half hour until it comes off the table (possibly marble which, even in a modern kitchen, should not be missing).

Put this dough, so worked, to rise in a salad bowl for two hours in a sheltered and not cold place (it should double its volume).

Subsequently divide the dough into two parts and gently roll out a part in a pan of 10.5 inch in diameter and 4 inch high, buttered and floured, being careful to spread it with wet hands and lightly sprinkling the dough with a little d 'water; this will help to prevent the padding from falling into the pasta.

Put the ham cut into strips, the diced scamorza, the squared béchamel and the peas; cover with the other dough and put the brioche to grow again until it has almost reached the edge of the pan.

Bake in the preheated oven at 350° F for about 30 minutes.

The brioche will finish growing in the oven and when cooked it will look splendid.

MUSHROOMS AND ARTICHOKES CREPES PASTRY

Ingredients for 8 people

For crepes: 6 eggs - flour 12 oz - ½ quart of milk - butter 2 oz - 3 spoons of parmesan - salt

For the filling: ½ quart of milk - flour 2 oz - butter 2 oz - 1 stock dice - grated Parmisan cheese 2 oz - fresh cultivated mushrooms 20 oz - 5 fresh artichokes - 1 bag of cooking cream - 3 tablespoons of oil - 1 woodpecker of garlic

PREPARATION

For the crepes, beat the eggs in a crepe and add the Parmesan, the milk, in which you have previously diluted the flour, and, passing it by pouring it on the eggs, from a small sieve; complete the mixture with the addition of the melted butter and salt.

Take a pan with an unassailable base of 7 inch in diameter and grease it with a cotton swab dipped in oil.

This operation must be repeated from time to time.

For each crepes, pour 2 and a half tablespoons of the mixture into the pan and slide it over the entire surface; the fire for cooking must be moderate.

Crepes must be thin and just golden brown.

Separately prepare the stuffing: the béchamel with half a liter of milk, the butter (2 oz), the flour (2 oz), salt to taste, with the nut the well cleaned mushrooms cut into slices for the long time sauté with oil (3 tablespoons) and browned garlic, well cleaned artichokes, cut in half and boiled for 7 minutes.

Then pass the artichokes from the chopper and add the cream bag to this cream. Take a baking pan with a diameter of 10 inch and another 2 inch, grease it and arrange 3 of the crepes: on these you have a spoonful of bechamel and spread it evenly, sprinkle the grated Parmisan cheese, a spoonful of mushrooms and, lastly, a spoonful of cream of artichokes with cream.

By following this order, proceed in the various layers until the crepes and ingredients run out.

On the surface, cover only with bechamel, cheese and a few flakes of butter. Bake your pastry in the oven at a temperature of 350° F and leave it for about 20 minutes to obtain a nice golden crust on the top.

It is a dish with a delicate flavor, very light, very pleasant on the palate which, given its characteristics, can also be served at an important dinner.

ARTICHOKE PIZZA

Ingredients for 8 people

For the shortcrust pastry: flour 16 oz - butter 4 oz - margarine 4 oz - ½ glass of hot water - salt to taste

For the filling: 10 artichokes - raw ham 3 oz - salami 5 oz - sweet provolone 6 oz - parmesan 4 oz - a pinch of pecorino - 3 whole eggs - 4 slices

PREPARATION

First of all, prepare the brisè pasta by placing the flour on the table with the butter, margarine and salt to taste; dry crumble these ingredients until the flour has absorbed all the fat and is reduced to small crumbs.

Pour the hot water on the mixture and mix; you will see that, in a short time, the dough will appear soft and velvety; give the pasta a few more strokes by beating it on the table and put it to rest.

In the meantime, prepare the padding: as a first operation, clean the artichokes, remove all the leathery part, cut them into small wedges that, floured, put to soak in acidulated water.

In a double-bottomed pan, which has an airtight seal, put 3 tablespoons of olive oil and a clove of garlic that you will brown; at this point pour the well washed artichokes (very white given the treatment they had) and cook them on a low heat with a covered pan.

If necessary, add a few tablespoons of water and cook them. In a large bowl, beat the eggs with the Parmesan cheese, salt and a pinch of pepper, if you like, add the ham cut into strips, the salami, also this thinly cut, the provolone cut into squares and the pinch of pecorino cheese.

Take a pan 10 inch in diameter and 2 inch high, and, after having greased and floured it, put a little more than half of the pastry in order to cover all the bottom and the edges.

Make a first layer of artichokes, on these a layer with the egg mixture and two slices cut in half, then repeat the layer of artichokes and mixture until exhaustion. Cover your cake with the rest of the dough and brush it on top with an egg yolk. With a fork, prick the surface of the cake to allow the humidity of the padding to come out without breaking and inflating the surface too much. Proceed to bake the cake at 350° F for about an hour.

This cake, which has all the flavor of spring, a cultured pie on the serving dish, should be served lukewarm to better enjoy its flavors.

It is very good for a dinner with friends.

SCAROLA'S PIZZA

Ingredients for 6 people

For the pasta: flour 12 oz - butter 3 oz - step 3 oz - sugar 5 oz - 3 egg yolks - salt - a few drops of milk

For the filling: _scarole_ (type of Italian vegetables) kg. 1 – ½ cup olive oil - Gaeta olives 4 oz - capers 1 oz - raisins and pine nuts 3 oz - 3 salted anchovies - 2 cloves of garlic

PREPARATION

Prepare the pastry as explained in the bottom of the recipe book and let it rest for about an hour in a tea towel in a cool and sheltered place.

Wash the scarole well (good cooking of a vegetable depends on washing it well), drain and throw it in boiling salted water (the water in the pot must not exceed three quarters of a liter).

Leave to cook for 4-5 minutes.

Climb the scarole and, once cooled, squeeze them very well to remove the bitterness.

In a pan, in which you will have put the oil, brown two cloves of garlic. Season the escarole in oil for about 10 minutes by adding the pitted olives, capers, raisins and pine nuts.

Finally, when the scarole is ready, add the washed, chopped anchovies out of the heat and remove the garlic.

In the buttered and floured baking pan with a diameter of 10 inch and 3 inch high, spread a little more than the shortcrust pastry, put the stuffing and cover the vegetables with a disk of dough the size of the pan, close the edges with a fork, brush with a egg yolk and bake.

The heat of the oven must be of an average temperature of 350° F and cooking will be complete after about an hour.

It is a typical Neapolitan dish, much appreciated and desired by those who have a so-called "thin palate"

PIZZA "PREGNANT"

Ingredients for 6 people

For the pasta: flour 12 oz - step 2 oz - 1 pack of beer yeast - salt to taste - half a cup of hot milk

For the filling: _fior di latte or scamorza_ (2 types of Italian cheese) 10 oz - 3 whole eggs - parmesan 4 oz - _mortadella_ (type of Italian ham) 5 oz - salt and pepper to taste

PREPARATION

Cold crumble the flour with the yeast, the step and the salt until the flour has absorbed both the yeast and the step and will have returned without lumps.

This small initial trick will facilitate the processing of the pasta, which once soaked with hot, but not boiling milk, will be soft and velvety.

Take a baking tray with a diameter of 10 inch, 2-3 inch high, and after having greased and floured it, cover it with a disk made from just over half the dough, about 0.4 inch thick.

Beat the crepes eggs and add the grated Parmesan, the diced scamorza cheese, the mortadella cut into strips, as well as the salt and pepper in the right size.

Put the stuffing in the prepared pan and cover the pizza with another smaller disc, but that completely covers the stuffing and with a fork close the edges.

110

Put to rise in a sheltered place and bake the pizza after about two and a half hours, on medium heat (350° F) for about 4 minutes.

You will see that the pizza in the oven will swell again and, once cooked, will give excellent results.

With the _friarielli_ (_type of Italian – better to say ... - a type of Naples' vegetable_) in oil and lemon it will be an excellent dinner.

RUSTIC PIZZA

Ingredients for 8 people

For the pasta: flour 12 oz - butter 3 oz - step 3 oz - sugar 5 oz - 3 egg yolks - a few drops of milk - salt

For the filling: hard cottage cheese 20 oz - 3 whole eggs - 1 yolk - parmesan 2 oz - cooked ham 4 oz - fior di latte (special Italian cheese) 8 oz - salt and pepper

For the bechamel: ½ quart of milk - butter 2 oz - flour 2 oz

PREPARATION

Prepare the shortcrust pastry by placing the flour on the table, the yolks, the butter cut into slices and kept first at room temperature, the step, the sugar and a pinch of salt.

Knead quickly and add a few drops of milk to get the pasta well mixed; when it detaches from the table and from your hands, place it in a tea towel in a cool, unventilated place.

Now let's go to the stuffing, pass the ricotta from the horsehair sieve, add the 3 eggs with the yolk to the crepe, the ham cut into strips, the fior di latte cut into squares, the béchamel previously prepared and mix everything.

Spread a little more than half of the dough on a sheet of floured greaseproof paper, turn it into the pan, keeping your arm under the paper, the diameter of the pan 10 inch and 3 inch high, put the padding, cover with the remaining dough from which you will have obtained a disk more or less the size of the pan.

Remove the pasta deficit and close the edges with a fork; with the remains of the dough, make some garnish on the surface of the pizza which will first be pricked on a fork, then brushed with an egg yolk.

You can finally put in the oven at 350° F and leave to cook for about 1 hour and a half.

You will see that the pizza will take on a magnificent appearance, it will be blonde, fragrant and shiny due to the presence of the brush of the egg yolk.

And ... enjoy your meal.

NAPLES' TORTANO

Ingredients for 8 people

For the pasta: flour 12 oz - suet 4 oz - 1 stick of beer leavened de 1 oz - salt to taste

For the filling: Neapolitan salami 4 oz - semi-spicy provolone 4 oz - greaves 4 oz - 2 boiled eggs

PREPARATION

To prepare the pasta put the flour on the table and, in the middle of it, half the lard with the other ingredients.

Initially crumble the ingredients dry in the flour until it has absorbed all of them. It will take about 10 minutes for this work and the more the flour will result in small crumbs, the better the result of the dough processing.

Add half a glass of hot, but not boiling water, and continue the processing for another 20 minutes so that the dough is elastic, during this process, beat it repeatedly on the table.

Finally, in a large bowl put the dough to grow for at least 2 hours until it has doubled in volume.

Separately prepare the stuffing by cooking the hard-boiled eggs and by cutting both the salami and the provolone in strips, while the eggs will be cut into wedges and chunks into chunks.

Spread a cloth on the table, flour it and, on this, spread the dough you will roll with a rolling pin to the thickness of 0.4 inch.

Brush the surface with the remaining suet and lay all the ready-made padding on it.

With the help of the tea towel, roll the dough on itself so as to obtain a nice roll that you will add in a shape with the central hole of the diameter of 10 inch and 2.7 inch high previously handled and floured; join the two ends of the roll and start growing again.

The second time the leavening should be shorter, in an hour and a half the tortano will have to reach almost the top of the pan. In the previously heated oven, bake the tortano at a temperature of 350° F and cooking will be completed after 45-50 minutes of cooking. Even if it is a tortano rich in ingredients, if the processing is performed to perfection, you will see that it will not be heavy, indeed it will be light and very much appreciated on the palate.

PASQUALINA SAVORED CAKE

Ingredients for 8 people

For the pasta: flour 14 oz - butter 6 oz - salt to taste

For the filling: 6 artichokes - fresh peas 40 oz or 1 box of frozen peas - 6 eggs - 4 tablespoons of grated Parmesan cheese - 1 handful of breadcrumbs soaked in milk - ricotta 14 oz – ½ cup olive oil - bacon 2 oz - 4 fresh onions - salt, pepper and nutmeg to taste

For the browning: 1 egg yolk

PREPARATION

First, prepare the dough using the usual system: put the flour on the table and, in the center of it, the butter kept at room temperature and cut into thin slices and the salt.

Dry crumble the ingredients until the flour has absorbed all the butter.

Add half a glass of hot water and work the pasta for 15 minutes until it becomes soft and velvety.

Put the pasta to rest and proceed with the padding.

Clean the artichokes and cut them into small wedges, flour them and keep them for about half an hour in acidified water.

In a saucepan, where you have put half a deciliter of oil, you will brown two onions, then add the well-washed and dried artichokes with a finger of glass of water.

At the beginning, for the first 10 minutes, cooking must take place with the pan covered, while you will complete the operation with the pan uncovered.

With the same system, cook the peas, putting the other 2 onions, the remaining oil and the well-chopped bacon. Pass the ricotta from the sieve, add the already cooked and cooled vegetables to it, 3 eggs, beaten with crepe with Parmesan, the breadcrumbs soaked in milk and then squeezed, salt, pepper and a pinch of nutmeg.

Divide the dough into two parts, one of which is larger, which you will spread on a disc and put it in a 10 inch diameter pan, buttered and floured.

Once the dough is spread over it, spread half of the padding.

At this point, in the padding, make 3 grooves at equal distances and, in these wells, gently pour 1 whole fresh egg, taking care not to break it.

Cover with the rest of the padding and complete the cake with the other dough that you will have also spread this disc.

Prick the surface with a fork and brown it by brushing the egg yolk on it. You can finally bake the cake at a temperature of 350° F and cook for 45-50 minutes.

All the scent of spring will be released when you serve it.

Enjoy your meal.

PRESERVES

ORANGE PRESERVES

Ingredients

Juicy oranges 120 oz (about 10 oranges) - water for half the weight of the oranges - sugar by weight equal to the oranges -1 lemon - 3-4 tablespoons of Rhum

PREPARATION

Take 10 rather large and juicy oranges and put them for 3 days in soaking in cold water after practicing 5-6 snags with a fork on each peel, taking care not to damage the pulp.

Every morning and every evening the water will have to be replaced, this operation is used to remove the bitterness.

After three days, remove the oranges from the water and peel them with a sharp knife, removing only the part of the peel and not the white bread.

Cut these peels into small strips.

Now remove the white of the oranges and cut them into thin slices removing the seeds.

Weigh these slices and peels and cook them with half the water of their weight and with the sugar equal to the weight itself.

Over moderate heat, cook the preserves for about 2 hours, turning always with a ladle of new wood.

The preserve will be ready when, by pouring a drop onto a plate, it does not expand.

Before removing from the heat, add the rum and put the preserves still hot in the glass jars, leaving them to cool for 24 hours with a cloth on top.

Closed the jars, always after putting the disk of greaseproof paper soaked in alcohol, the preserve will be ready to be stored or consumed.

The lemon put in the ingredients will be optional.

This preserve is no less than the lemon preserve and is well suited for use in excellent tarts.

LEMON PRESERVES

Ingredients

12 medium-sized lemons - sugar 60 oz

PREPARATION

This preserve is widely used in both France and England for its delicate flavor. Remove the skins from the 12 lemons and cut them into thin strips. Instead, you will cut the lemons into slices by removing all the seeds.

On the 1st day, put the lemons with the skins in a large container and cover them with water.

On the 2nd day pour everything into a pot (including the water of the day before) and bring to the boil by boiling for 10 minutes. Let the lemons rest in their water for another 24 hours.

On the 3rd day, drain the lemons by throwing their water; add 10 glasses of water and put them on the fire; bring to a boil and leave to cook for 20 minutes to give the skins time to soften.

Drain the lemons again and, of the liquid, take only 8 glasses that you will put on the fire with the sugar, boiling for 10 minutes to obtain a nice syrup.

At this point add the lemons and cook for about 2 hours on a low heat, stirring constantly. The preserve will be ready to be put in the jars that you will leave open overnight. With this procedure, the humidity will go away and all that remains will be to cover the surface of the preservation with a disk of greaseproof paper soaked in alcohol.

The color of this preserves will be amber blonde, with a delicate flavor, while the lemons will have lost their sour and bitter taste, leaving only the scent.

CHESTNUT JAM

Ingredients

Chestnuts 80 oz - sugar 96 oz - water quart 0.75 - 2 sachets of vanilla

PREPARATION

Take the chestnuts and remove the brown skin from them and cook them in abundant lightly salted water until they are cooked (about 40 minutes).

Drain the chestnuts, remove the skin and pass them through a horsehair sieve, taking care of massing the past dough with your hands.

Separately, take the sugar with the water and put it in a triple-bottomed steel pot, bring to the boil and let it boil gently for 10 minutes.

Only then can you add the chestnut puree with the vanilla sachets, taking care to cook over a very low heat and stirring constantly; 40 minutes or so should be enough for cooking.

The jam will have to take on a darker, shiny and transparent color and will be ready to be put in the jars that you will leave uncovered for 24 hours.

As with all jams, cover the surface of the jars with a disc of greaseproof paper soaked in alcohol and close tightly.

It is a very nutritious jam, because it is rich in sugar and carbohydrates, which will be the joy of your children and, apart from this, the use for sweets is manifold.

.

SWEET COOKIE CREAMS

BABBA'

Ingredients for 12 people

Flour 19 oz - 8 fresh eggs - butter 6 oz - brewer's yeast 2 oz - 1 pinch of salt - sugar 2 oz for the syrup: 1 quart and a half of water - sugar 26 oz - 5 lemon peels – ½ glass of rum.

PREPARATION

The day before the preparation of the dessert, prepare the syrup, putting the water with the sugar and the skins of the 5 lemons in a saucepan; boil and cook over moderate heat for 40 minutes.

The syrup will acquire a yellowish color, so as soon as it has cooled, pass it through a cloth in a salad bowl that will remain covered until the next day. To make the babà, put the flour, the sliced butter, the eggs, the yeast, the sugar, the salt in a salad bowl and mix it with your hands.

If you have a medium-sized mixer, transfer the dough to this, let the processing go on for half an hour, that is, until the dough comes off the walls.

If you want to do the work by hand, which is perhaps better and more reason for pride, transfer the dough to a marble table, which I hope you have, and beat vigorously for a good half hour until it detaches from the table and hands.

Put the dough to rise in the salad bowl for two and a half hours, until the volume has doubled.

128

Take a shape with a diameter of about 11 inch with a central hole that will have a diameter of about 2.7 inch, butter it and flour it well, arrange the dough by spoonfuls without scrambling it very much, in the shape, matching the surface well with a damp spoon.

When the dough has reached the top of the shape, heat the oven and then bake the cake at a temperature of 400° F.

Halfway through cooking, when the babà has taken on a nice biscuit color on the surface, you can decrease the temperature to 350° F.

It will not take more than half an hour to cook this splendid dessert, as the pasta is very light.

Take the babà out of the oven with a sieve of horsehair, and place a plate underneath which will collect the syrup not absorbed by the cake.

Pour the cold syrup on the hot babà trying to wet all the sides; continue this operation until the cake has absorbed all the syrup.

Finally, wet the dessert again, before serving it, with the rum that must be the red one.

What could be more pleasing to us Neapolitans than a babà but done in order? Although the origins of this dessert are not from our beautiful Naples, I think it is the most traditional dessert, whose name alone will give such importance, and there will be no guest who will not be liked.

.

RUSTIC BABBA'

Ingredients for 6 people

Potatoes 12 oz - flour 12 oz - brewer's yeast 2 oz - 2 whole eggs

For the filling: 1 whole egg - 1 tablespoon of Parmesan - raw ham 4 oz - provola (type of Italian cheese) 4 oz

PREPARATION

This recipe, which was given to me by a dear friend, is worth considering.

These rustic babà, if successful, will be soft, crisp and tasty; in a family they will disappear in the blink of an eye, especially if you have children who are still young.

Boil the potatoes which must be of good quality, the yellow ones; in the meantime, dissolve the brewer's yeast in a sip of warm milk.

Mix the flour with the eggs, a pinch of salt, the dissolved yeast and the potatoes passed in the potato masher.

Knead the dough, but not very much, until you have obtained a soft paste; then let it rise in a bowl for about two hours (the volume should double). On the well-floured table, roll out the dough to a height of one centimeter.

Aside you will have already prepared the filling with the whole beaten egg, the parmesan, the ham cut into strips and the diced provola.

With a glass of wine, make many discs from the dough and, with the leftovers that you re-knead, still make the last discs until exhaustion.

The disks should be 32, as the babas with these proportions should be 16.

On 16 disks, arrange the filling equally, cover with the other disks and press the edges of each babà with your fingers; the soft paste will facilitate the operation. Let it grow for another hour and, in a pan with plenty of oil, preferably sunflower, fry the babas at medium temperature; they will swell beautifully and become a beautiful golden color. Let them cook for at least 6-7 minutes so they can also be cooked inside.

You can fry in a rather large pan three at a time.

They are served hot and ... enjoy your meal.

WHITE EAT FIRST WAY

Ingredients for 5 people

½ quart of milk - sweet starch 2 oz - sugar 6 oz - the peel of 1 lemon - 1 sachet of vanilla - candied pumpkin 2 oz - dark chocolate 2 oz

PREPARATION

Dissolve the starch in cold milk and pass it through a colander to avoid a few small lumps of starch.

Add sugar, lemon peel, vanilla bag to the mixture and cook over low heat, stirring constantly.

After about 10 minutes of cooking, you will see that the cream has consolidated in the right way and you can remove it from the heat to let it cool.

Add the candied pumpkin cut into pieces and the fondant also cut into pieces. Arrange the cream in slightly wet cups and put them in the refrigerator for 5-6 hours. after the time, turn the cream of each cup on the saucers and garnish with a candied cherry.

It is a very light dessert suitable for children and also and above all for elderly people who must not be forgotten.

BOMBOLONI

Ingredients for 6 people

Flour 12 oz - butter 2 oz - brewer's yeast 1 oz - 1 whole egg - 2 yolks - sugar 1 oz - the grater of 1 lemon - ½ Brandy shell - lukewarm milk ½ cup

For the cream: milk 10 oz - 2 yolks - flour 1 oz - sugar 2 oz - 1 lemon peel - black cherries in jam 6 oz

PREPARATION

Put the flour on the table and, in the center of it, the yeast, butter, salt, sugar and crumble these ingredients dry until the flour has absorbed them all.

At this point, add the egg with the 2 yolks, the Brandy and the lukewarm milk little by little, until you get a soft paste that you will work for about 20 minutes.

Put the dough to grow in a bowl and when it has reached the top of the bowl, spread this gently on the table, then spreading it with a rolling pin up to a thickness of 0.6 inch.

Obtain from this dough many discs that you will cut with a glass.

Knead the dough, stay and repeat the operation until exhaustion.

Still grow your donuts which you will cover with a cloth for about 40 minutes. In a pan with plenty of sunflower oil, fry over medium heat and you will see that they will swell wonderfully.

As soon as the donuts are lukewarm, give each of them a lateral incision with scissors to introduce a spoonful of cream and another of black cherry.

When the operation is completed, place them on a serving dish and sprinkle them with plenty of icing sugar.

These are the classic "BOMBOLONI TOSCANI", light, pleasant and very appetizing.

RICE PUDDING

Ingredients for 8 people

For the shortcrust pastry: flour 12 oz - butter 5 oz - salt - ½ glass of hot water

For the filling: rice 12 oz - milk 1.25 quart - sugar 8 oz - butter 4 oz - pumpkin and candied orange 3 oz - 3 whole eggs - 2 yolks - the grated peel of 1 orange - vanilla icing sugar 2 oz

PREPARATION

Prepare the shortcrust pastry by placing the flour on the table with the butter cut into small slices and a pinch of salt.

Dry crumble the butter with the salt in the flour and continue this operation for about 10 minutes until the mixture is well chopped into very small crumbs.

 At this point you can add the hot water and you will see that, for the previous processing, the dough will turn out, after kneading it and working it for a short time, soft and velvety.

Cover the dough with a cloth and let it rest for about 2 hours.

For the stuffing, boil the milk with the rice, the grated orange, the sugar, the butter and cook for at least 40-50 minutes until the mixture appears as a thick cream and the rice grains are almost no longer they will be seen.

Whilst you let it cool, whisk the 3 egg whites until stiff.

Once cooled, add the 5 egg yolks, the pumpkin and the candied orange cut into small pieces to the mixture, and, little by little while mixing, the egg whites beaten until stiff. In a baking pan 10 inch in diameter and 2.4 inch high, buttered and floured, arrange the shortcrust pastry so that it is about 0.1 inch thick.

Add the filling on top, garnishing the surface with two strips obtained from the advanced pasta, 0.4 inch and a half wide, cross-shaped, while on the whole edge you will put a roll of pasta the thickness of the little finger.

Put in the oven and cook the cake for at least 50 minutes at 350° F.

Remove from the oven and, once lukewarm, pulverize it with vanilla icing sugar. It is a very delicate dessert, very suitable for both children and elderly people, but why not for everyone?

This dessert is widely used in Tuscany where, in all pastry shops, you will find rice puddings packed in small oval shapes.

CASSATA ALLA SICILIANA

Ingredients for 8 people

Sponge cake: packaged with 5 eggs

For the filling: Roman ricotta 20 oz - sugar 14 oz - dark 3 oz - cocoa 4 oz - cedar and candied orange 4 oz

For wetting: ¾ cup water - sugar 2 oz - the peel of 1 orange - 1 small glass of Brandy

For the cover: ½ jar of apricot jelly - candied cherries 4 oz - 1 candied mandarin - _naspro_ (see the recipe in this book) with 12 oz of sugar

PREPARATION

Prepare a sponge cake as per the recipe in this recipe book but since there are 5 eggs, use a 10 inch diameter and 2 inch high pan.

Therefore, pass the ricotta from a horsehair sieve and mix the sugar with it, working the dough until the sugar has dissolved.

To your liking you can add a few spoonfuls of orange blossom water to the cream, but this is practically optional, add the cocoa leaving aside a third that will serve as a garnish, the dark chocolate, also cut into minutes, as well as cedar and candied orange which will have the same treatment.

Prepare the syrup with water and sugar by boiling 6-7 minutes, lastly add the brandy.

Cut the sponge cake into two discs, wet the first disc with the ready-made and cold syrup.

Before this operation, if the thickness of the sponge cake is too thick, in the center of the disc dig a little by removing the crumbs that they will come out.

Arrange the ricotta cream, cover it with the other disc also wet with the syrup. Spread the fruit jelly on the cake and on this the naspro which will be well balanced even on the edges with a long blade knife.

To facilitate the task, put strips of greaseproof paper on the serving plate before placing the first disk on them, but they will remain a little outside the edges, when you have completed with the naspro, pull them gently and the edges will remain completely clean.

As a final touch, place the cocoa, cherries and the candied mandarin on display in the center. Prepare this dessert a few days before use, so that all the flavors can merge (the lower part of the refrigerator will be very good for storage).

The packaging of this dessert is a bit laborious, although not difficult, but your work will be worthily compensated by the enthusiasm of all those who will be lucky enough to taste it.

"CHIACCHIERE"

Ingredients for 8 people

12 oz flour - 2 eggs - 2 tablespoons of sugar - 1 small glass of Brandy - 2 tablespoons of sunflower oil - the grated 1 lemon - salt

PREPARATION

Put the flour on the table and in the center add the whole eggs with all the ingredients.

Knead to make the dough soft; if the dough is too hard you can add a few drops of milk.

Work the dough on the table, beating it for about 20 minutes, and then put it to rest for about an hour.

Spread the dough (it will be better to do it in two stages) in two thin sheets of a thickness of about 0.08 inch and with the wheel cut the diamond lozenges and fry in plenty of hot oil.

As you remove the small talk from the oil you will drain it on a sheet of absorbent paper, then you can serve them covered with vanilla icing sugar.

CREAM CARAMEL

Ingredients for 6 people

Milk 1 quart - sugar 4 oz - 4 whole eggs - 2 yolks - the peel of 1 lemon - 1 sachet of vanilla - sugar for the caramel 5 oz

PREPARATION

Boil the milk with the sugar and the lemon peel over a very low heat (so that the milk does not come out of the milk jug, introduce a steel spoon into it) for about 30 minutes; the milk with this procedure will shrink a little and is the result we want to get. In a shape, 7.5 inch in diameter and 4 inch high, put the caramelized sugar to caramelize; the latter must reach the extreme cooking point of a very dark brown color, with a perfume that will remind you of bitter almond.

Slide the caramel over the entire internal wall of the mold until it is completely coated and let cool.

Separately whip the whole eggs with the yolks (crepe type) and mix this with the cooled milk. Pour the mixture into a form through a colander.

Take the latter and put it in a larger pan half-filled with water to cook in a water bath in the oven at 350° F for about 50 minutes.

Before baking, cover the container containing the cream with a well-sealed aluminum foil.

When cooked, allow the cake to cool then put it in the refrigerator for 5-6 hours; at this point it is ready to be baked and served with its magnificent sauce.

The contrast of the cream dessert with the bitterness of the caramel and its lightness makes this dessert one of the best I know.

Try it and you'll agree with me.

ENGLISH CREAM

Ingredients for 6 people

Half a quart of milk - 5 egg yolks - sugar 6 oz - 2 sachets of vanilla

PREPARATION

Beat the egg yolks with the sugar until it becomes a thick and frothy cream; pour hot milk over it with the addition of 2 sachets of vanilla.

Put the mixture on the fire and cook in a bain-marie on a very low heat, taking the utmost care that even the water in the bain-marie must only simmer otherwise the cream could tear.

Cooking must last for about an hour and the cream will be ready when it leaves a veil on the wooden spoon that you have used to continuously turn the preparation in the same direction throughout the cooking time.

Note: the English cream will be kept in the fridge before use.

PASTRY CREAM

Ingredients for 6 people

Milk 20 oz - 4 yolks - flour 2 oz - sugar 5 oz - the peel of 1 lemon

PREPARATION

In a large bowl, beat the egg yolks with the sugar until you get a thick cream that will have to go down in a ribbon if you lift the spoon. In another bowl put the flour and add to it, little by little, the cold milk, turning vigorously so that no lumps are created.

Pass the mixture through a strainer on the beaten eggs and turn everything cold. It will be time to put the cream with the lemon peel in a saucepan and bring it on the heat with moderate heat.

The cream must never rise to a boil; cook for about 15 minutes and you will see that, at the right time, this will thicken.

It will be preferable to continue occasionally turning the cream out of the heat until it is lukewarm; this is to prevent a tougher film from forming on the surface. Before letting it cool completely put a little butter on the surface.

Finally, you can use it at your convenience, eating it "_au naturel_" or used to garnish other desserts.

ANANAS FLAN WITH ENGLISH CREAM

Ingredients for 8 people

1 box of pineapple 34 oz - 6 eggs - sugar 6 oz - 1 tablespoon of flour - juice of 1 lemon - 1 small glass of kirsc

For the caramel: sugar 4 oz

PREPARATION

Open the box of pineapples, take all the washers except one, which you will keep aside for the garnish, and pass them with the chopper until they are homogeneous.

Now take three quarters of the syrup contained in the box and add it to the sugar by putting this mixture to boil for 10 minutes.

Separately, in a small cup, dilute the flour with the lemon juice.

After these operations, let's move on to the preparation of the cake: take a shape with a diameter of 8 inch and 3 inch high. and pour the 4 oz.

Sugar that you will caramelize on the fire with the addition of a few tablespoons of water, until you get a nice blonde color; the caramel must line the inside of the shape.

Now beat the eggs in a bowl for 5 minutes and add the prepared pineapple pulp, the flour diluted with lemon, the syrup and the glass of Kirsc.

Pour this mixture into the form and bake at 350° F in a water bath for about an hour.

When cooked, make sure that the cake cools down and put it in the fridge without turning it out for at least 5-6 hours.

Now that you can say that you have reached the finish line, because now the flan is ready and can be easily deformed showing a beautiful caramelized appearance with a magnificent sauce left by it.

Decorate the flan with the pineapple washer that you will have well protected from some family gluttony and, as a final touch, a cherry in the hole in the washer.

This dessert should be accompanied with the delicious English cream that you will serve in a separate tray.

ORANGE GATEAU

Ingredients for 6 people

4 eggs - sugar 7 oz - flour 6 oz - 6 tablespoons of seed oil - ½ sachet of yeast - the grater of 1 orange peel - the juice of an orange and a half

PREPARATION

Work the reds with the sugar, preferably using the electric whisk; when the mixture appears clear and frothy, add the oil, the sifted flour with the yeast, the grated orange peel, and the juice, alternating the ingredients until obtaining a soft mixture that must appear as a thick cream.

Aside, whisk the egg whites until stiff and add them little by little and gently.

In a 8.6 inch diameter and 4 inch high shape, greased and floured, arrange the mixture and put it in the oven at 350° F for about an hour.

The cake will grow wonderfully and will be very light, also suitable for elderly people and for those who must follow a diet.

MONT BLANC

Ingredients for 6 people

Chestnuts 20 oz - ½ glass of milk - sugar 4 oz - cocoa 2 oz - 1 sachet of vanilla - whipped cream 16 oz

PREPARATION

Remove the outer skin of the chestnuts then, in abundant slightly salted water to enhance the flavor, cook them.

Once cooked, free the chestnuts from the second peel and pass them in the horsehair sieve.

Put everything to cook for about 10 minutes with the sugar, cocoa, milk, vanilla, stirring constantly and on a very low heat.

At this point let the puree cool completely and, on the serving plate which must be round, pass the puree again so that it will no longer appear massed but light, because it will have broken down into many small vermicelli.

All you have to do is cover this mound of chestnuts with the whipped cream. It is ultimately a very simple dessert whose combinations of flavors will make it very refined and certainly successful.

In autumn this dessert will also worthily complete an important dinner.

NASPRO

For a 10 inch diameter cake

Ingredients

Sugar 12 oz - 2 fingers of water - 1 pinch of baking soda - the grated peel of 1 lemon - a few drops of lemon

PREPARATION

Put the sugar with the water and a pinch of baking soda in a saucepan, boil on the fire.

You will see a thick white foam form when the syrup boils.

Continuing with the cooking instead of the white foam, large transparent bubbles will form, it means that the cooking of the _naspro_ (see the recipe in this book) starts at the right point.

Take a drop of the mixture and if you feel it sticking between your fingers, the naspro is ready for the last processing.

Pour the mixture, preferably in a marble mortar, otherwise in a sturdy bowl that you previously kept in the refrigerator for half an hour.

Let the syrup cool down and when you see that a very light plate has formed on the top, start turning pouring a few drops of lemon every now and then.

The syrup will soon turn white as snow.

148

The naspro is ready and you just have to pour it on the cake.

NEGRETTI

Ingredients

Dry biscuits - OROSAIVA in Italy are perfect!!! - (5 oz) - cocoa 2 oz - butter 2 oz - mascarpone 4 oz - 1 egg yolk - 4 tablespoons of cognac - icing sugar 5 oz - chocolate grain 3 oz

PREPARATION

Of these soft chocolates, which melt in your mouth, you will have to make many if you want someone to remain for your husband when he returns from work.

The processing is simple but must be done carefully; beat the butter with the sugar well, add the egg yolk and continue processing.

Little by little you will complete the dough first by putting the mascarpone (it must be compact) then the cocoa, the finely shredded biscuits, alternating the latter ingredients with cognac.

Put the dough in the fridge for it to firm up and form the negretti the size of an acorn, pass them in the chocolate chips and put the paper baking cups to each.

They should be kept in a tightly closed tin box that should be kept in the fridge. They are removed from the fridge just before use.

QUICKLY EXECUTED SPONGE CAKE

Ingredients for 8 people

8 fresh whole eggs - 8 spoons of flour with potato starch in the right proportion - 8 spoons of sugar - a few drops of lemon - the grater of 1 lemon - 1 sachet of vanilla

PREPARATION

Divide the reds from the whites and set the yolks aside in a bowl.

Beat the egg whites until stiff, to which you will add a few drops of lemon and, little by little, the sugar.

When the dough is well assembled, put the egg yolks one at a time.

Finally, with a wooden spoon, gently add the flour mixed with the starch, the grated lemon, as well as the vanilla sachet to the mixture. In a baking pan 11 inch in diameter and 3 inch high, buttered and floured, arrange the mixture that can pass to the oven, first heated, at a temperature of 350° F, 45 minutes will be enough for cooking and a knitting needle will confirm it.

Once inserted in the cake, it must come out clean.

To facilitate the growth of the dessert, it will not be bad to add a teaspoon of baking powder to the dough before cooking.

The execution, as you can see, will be simple and the result excellent.

With this system the cake will not lower or shrink, only the edges will detach slightly from the pan.

Lastly, in order not to give moisture to the cake, turn it out on a sieve.

PANDORO

Ingredients for 8 people

Flour 12 oz - sugar 3 oz - 1 whole egg - 4 yolks - butter 9 oz - ½ glass of milk - beer yeast 1 oz - 3 sachets of vanilla - icing sugar 4 oz

PREPARATION

Dilute the yeast with 2 oz of the flour of the ingredients and a few spoonfuls of warm milk, forming a small panel that you will let grow for about 40 minutes (in this time it should double in volume).

On the table put the other part of the flour (4 oz) and in the center put the leavened panel, the whole egg, an yolk, half the sugar of the doses and a knob of butter.

Mix everything and knead it for about 10 minutes, then put it in a floured bowl and put it to grow in a cool and sheltered place for an hour and a half.

After this time the dough will have doubled in volume.

Put the remaining flour (6 oz)

On the table and, in the center of it, put the leavened dough, the remaining 3 yolks, the remaining sugar, the butter, a sachet of vanilla and work everything for another 10 minutes.

The dough will appear well supported, soften it with the warm milk, the rest of the half glass, in order to obtain a soft dough that you will have to work for 30 minutes more.

Then let it grow in a capable tureen for at least 3 hours.

Gently place the dough on the table then, first with your hands then with a rolling pin, obtain a rectangle of 9x12 inch and a thickness of 0.4 inch. In the center of this rectangle put 7 oz of butter kept at room temperature and cut into small slices; place it regularly in the center.

Fold the first part of the pasta rectangle over the butter and, on this, the other part of the rectangle in order to obtain a bag that you will close both on the long side and on the two short sides.

Flour the table and with a rolling pin again get a rectangle with the same measurements as the previous one, fold again in three and, always helping yourself with the flour, spread the dough again; folded again but on the different side from the previous one.

At this point, without spreading the dough, let it rest covered for about an hour.

Take back the dough, spread it out and give two more turns as done previously, once on one side and once on the other.

Finally roll the rectangle dough on itself, twist it into shape and arrange it in the shape (diameter 7 inch, height 5 inch) abundantly buttered and sprinkled with vanilla icing sugar (2 oz).

Grow the pandoro all night and you will see that in the morning it will have reached the top of the form.

Bake with an initial temperature of 350° F and leave to cook for about two hours. You will see that after about 10 minutes of cooking the pandoro will still grow forming a nice hat.

When the surface is well colored, decrease the oven to 300° for the other cooking time.

Finally, you will only have to bake your cake and sprinkle it with vanilla icing sugar and serve it.

PANESIGLIO

Ingredients for 8 people

Flour 24 oz - sugar 2 oz - step 4 oz - 3 whole eggs – ½ cup milk - brewer's yeast 1 oz - grated lemon - 1 sachet of vanilla

PREPARATION

Sift the flour; take 6 oz of this and with lukewarm milk and yeast, make a soft cake to rise for 2 hours.

Take the rest of the flour and add the leavened cake with all the ingredients to it. You will have a soft dough that you will have to work for a good quarter of an hour by repeatedly beating it on the table.

Put the dough to rise in a large bowl for another two hours (in the winter in a slightly warm oven).

After the second growth, resume the dough, roll it out and wrap it on itself to obtain a long salami whose ends will be joined together, giving it the shape of a donut.

Now lay the dough in a buttered and floured baking pan with a diameter of 11 inch and 4 inch high and let it rise for a third time. Before putting it in the oven, when the cake has almost reached the top of the edges, brush it with an egg yolk, not forgetting to sprinkle it with granulated sugar as well.

The oven, previously heated, must have a temperature of 350° F and cooking will be complete after 45 minutes.

It is a very old date cake that, during my childhood as I remember, was often offered to my father by the cloistered nuns of a convent.

Excellent for breakfast and for your children's snack. If the results are satisfactory, the panesiglio must come well swollen while the central hole must disappear completely.

PASTIERA

Ingredients for 10 people

Shortcrust pastry: flour 16 oz - sugar 7 oz (finely chopped) - suet (butter and lard) 7 oz – 4 egg oxidation - ½ cognac eggshell - grated 1 lemon.

Filling: ricotta 20 oz - wheat 10 oz – 1 ½ cup of milk - 6 whole eggs minus 2 egg whites - cocoa and orange 3 oz - sugar 12 oz - grated lemon - 2 tablespoons of orange blossom water.

PREPARATION

Cook the wheat with milk, an orange peel and a knob of butter, for 40 minutes, until the milk is completely absorbed.

Prepare the shortcrust pastry by placing the flour, the suet, the egg yolks, the cognac, the sugar, a pinch of salt and the grated 1 lemon on the table.

Knead for a short time, until the dough is detached from the hands and the table. I use finely chopped sugar for the shortcrust pastry to have a more delicate mixture.

Therefore put the dough covered by a cloth in a cool, sheltered place for at least 2 hours.

Prepare the filling by beating the egg yolks with the sugar for about 20 minutes, until the mixture is white and frothy, add the ricotta that you have passed through a sieve of horsehair, candied peel, flower water and the wheat, half of which you will have passed through the sieve.

At the end you can add the egg whites whipped until stiff.

Take the shortcrust pastry and, with more than half of it, roll out a sheet on a sheet of waxed and greased paper.

In a pan 10 inch in diameter and about 2.3 inch high, greased and floured, roll up the pastry by placing your arm under the sheet, thus preventing the pastry from breaking.

With the prepared mixture, fill the pan and with the other dough, make lozenges that you will grill on the cake.

At the edges, put a roll of dough the thickness of a little finger and with a round tip knife, hollow all around, so as to obtain that the pastiera is well packaged.

Preheat the oven in advance, about 15 minutes, and informed the pastiera at an average temperature of about 325° F for baked for about 1 hour and a half.

The proof of the knitting needle introduced in the pastiera, and which must come out clean, will give you confirmation of a good cooking.

I advise you to prepare the pastiera 4-5 days before.

The flavors will merge, the pastiera will be more humid and all the more pleasing to the palate.

In this typical Easter cake we will feel all the scent of spring and the scent of Naples: it is the most famous Neapolitan Easter cake.

PASTIERA (in another way)

Ingredients for 10 people

Shortcrust pastry: flour 12 oz - margarine 5 oz - 2 egg yolks - sugar 4 oz - a few drops of milk

For the filling: wheat 10 oz - ricotta 16 oz - sugar 14 oz - 5 whole eggs minus 1 egg white - candied (cedar, orange) 6 oz - flower water a few spoonfuls

For the cream: milk 10 oz - 2 egg yolks - flour 2 oz - sugar 4 oz - the peel of a lemon

PREPARATION

First prepare the shortcrust pastry and to facilitate the task, work the margarine with the sugar to obtain a frothy dough; one at times add the egg yolks and finally the flour with the milk (two spoonfuls will suffice).

For this last operation, and that is when you add it you will do it with milk, the processing will have to be short, but you will see that given the previous processing the pasta will detach easily from the table and from your hands.

While the dough rests in a sheltered place, prepare the padding.

Cook the wheat in a saucepan covered with milk, a knob of butter and an orange peel for about 35 minutes on a low heat, until the milk has absorbed.

Pass the ricotta from the sieve, beat the egg yolks with the sugar to obtain a thick and frothy cream, add the ricotta, the wheat, the orange blossom water, the candied fruit cut into very small pieces and the cream you will have prepared with the same system as the recipe for custard.

Finally, you will complete the dough with whites that will be whipped, but not when the snow is still firm. In a 12 inch diameter and 1.6 inch high baking tray, greased and floured, arrange the shortcrust pastry sheet which you will have spread on a sheet of greaseproof paper, so that by turning it over in the pan it will not break, add the padding and complete with arrange the remaining striped dough cut with the diamond wheel.

At the edge put a small roll of dough that can cover the whole circumference and sprinkle the edges with a round knife.

Bake the pastiera at a temperature of 350° F and let it cook for just over an hour. This dessert will also be prepared a few days in advance and will not be less than the other recipe I have given you, but lighter and more suitable for those who must follow a diet.

ROCCOCO'

Ingredients for 24 Rococo

Flour 20 oz - sugar 20 oz - ½ glass of cold water - almonds 10 oz - 12 cloves - ½ grated nutmeg - 1 sachet of cinnamon powder - ½ stick of cinnamon - the grated peel of 1 orange - the grated peel of 1 lemon - 1 teaspoon pepper - salt - ammonium carbonate 2

PREPARATION

Gather all the ingredients on the table: the flour, sugar and all the aromas that you will have well crushed in a mortar, while at the end you will add the grated orange and lemon.

Mix all the dry ingredients and add the water little by little.

Work the dough a little (the presence of sugar will not allow it) and lastly add the ammonium carbonate, then give the dough a final kneading.

Let it rest overnight in a cool, sheltered place by covering it with a tea towel. Meanwhile, take the almonds, clean them with a cloth and toast them in the oven at moderate heat for about 15 minutes.

After the dough has rested for the necessary time, mix the whole almonds with it and form many sticks the thickness of a finger and the length of 4.8 inch; join the ends of the sticks by welding the two meeting points with your hands.

Brush the Roccocò with a freshly diluted egg yolk in a drop of milk and bake them about 0.8 inch apart.

In medium-sized home ovens, no more than 12 will go on the freshly buttered plate.

The heat of the oven must initially be at most 475° F to allow the Roccocò to swell and consolidate; after 7-8 minutes you can decrease the heat to 350° F.

Cooking should be complete after 20 minutes.

As soon as the Roccocòs are all ready to last for a certain time, put them back in the oven to bake at very moderate heat, 100° F, for a few hours.

I could not fail to offer you also this typical Christmas cake that you will gladly eat accompanied by a good sweet wine on long winter evenings.

SACHER CAKE

Ingredients for 8 people

For the pasta: dark chocolate 5 oz - butter 4 oz - flour 8 oz - sugar 8 oz - 5 eggs - ½ sachet of baking powder - 2 tablespoons of milk

For the filling: dark chocolate 6 oz - 4 tablespoons of fruit jelly - ½ cup of coffee

PREPARATION

Take a bowl of solid porcelain and put the dark chocolate with the butter in it.

Put the bowl in a pan where you have boiled 2 quart of water and allow the chocolate and butter to soften in a water bath.

Off the heat, add the sugar a little at a time and whisk these ingredients until you have obtained a light and frothy dough.

At this point, continue the process by adding the egg yolks one at a time and you will see that the mixture will increase in volume, thanks to the eggs that you will gradually add.

Complete the process by adding the sifted flour with the yeast and the two spoonfuls of milk.

Aside, beat the egg whites until stiff and add them to the dough gently.

You just have to place it in a buttered and floured baking pan with a diameter of 10 inch at a height of 2.8 inch.

Bake the cake at a temperature of 350° F (the oven will have to be previously heated) for about 45-50 minutes.

Meanwhile, prepare the cover by placing the fondant and butter in a bain-marie bowl to soften.

Off the heat, work the cream and add half a cup of coffee to it.

Divide the cake into two disks and on the first, after having smeared it with half of the jelly, put a little less than half of the cream, cover with the other disk, spread the remaining jelly again and "last but not least" the cream.

This is a classy dessert of Austrian origin and which will be counted among the highlights of the pastry shop.

It is delicious, delicate and would never tire of tasting it. Seeing is believing.

ENGLISH SALAMI

Ingredients for 16 people

For the basic pasta: 5 whole eggs - 5 tablespoons of sugar - 5 tablespoons of flour mixed with potato starch - a few drops of lemon

For the filling: butter 8 oz - sugar 10 oz - 4 egg yolks - 1 cup of coffee - Apart from 8 teaspoons of jam (apricot or black cherry)

For the syrup: ½ cup of water - 3 tablespoons of sugar - 1 glass of Strega liqueur - 1 glass of Rhum

PREPARATION

This dessert has no difficulty problems in its execution, it is very refined and has a very delicate flavor; you can count it in the "important" desserts and also prepare it for some occasion.

You will make a good impression!

For the basic dough: beat the egg whites of the 5 eggs until stiff and gradually add the sugar while continuing to knead the dough (with the electric whisk it will be much easier). Then add the egg yolks, also a little at a time, while lastly complete the processing with the addition of flour and starch.

On the oven plate, buttered and floured, place the mixture well laid out (height 0.6 inch) to obtain a rectangle. Bake at 350° F , 20 minutes of cooking will be enough.

Gently put this rectangle of sponge cake on a well-wrung wet cloth and cover with another well-wrung wet cloth.

For the filling: cut the butter into thin slices, which you will have kept out of the refrigerator at room temperature for at least half an hour, and put it in a bowl with the sugar to work it until it is light and frothy; a teaspoon at a time add the egg yolks and make sure that the mixture absorbs the egg well gradually.

The cream with the presence of eggs will increase in volume and finally you will put, even this little by little, the cup of coffee.

The cream will be ready, the important thing is to add both eggs and coffee in small doses, this to prevent it from tearing.

For the syrup: put the water in a saucepan and put all the ingredients (3 tablespoons of sugar, 1 glass of Strega liqueur and 1 glass of Rhum), and boil for 6-7 minutes

For the confection of the dessert you can cut the rectangle of sponge cake into two rectangles and, after having wet them with the cold syrup, you will spread over half the cream and 4 teaspoons of jam.

With the help of the tea towel, roll the two rectangles over themselves and put them on serving dishes.

Spread the two rolls with the remaining cream which will be more than abundant. Make spiral grooves or with a cake comb or fork and, after pulverizing the coffee powder on the cake, put everything in the refrigerator.

It will be preferable to pack the cake the day before use, the various flavors will merge better and the slices will be cut more compact.

SANGUINACCIO

Ingredients for 8 people

Half a quart of pig blood - milk 0,75 quart - starch 3 oz - flour 2 oz - butter 2 oz - lard 2 oz - bitter cocoa 4 oz - dark chocolate 3 oz - sugar 12 oz - cocoa and cedar 3 oz - 2 spoons of Rhum - 1 lemon peel - 1 sachet of cinnamon.

PREPARATION

From three quarters of milk, remove two cups, in one cold dilute the starch, in the other dilute the flour; add all the milk by passing it through a sieve.

Add the pig blood and go over all the liquid for the sieve again, to be sure that there are no blood clots or impurities.

At this point put the mixture in a pan with the cocoa, the dark chocolate, the sugar, the butter, the lard and the lemon peel. Bring the pan to the heat and let the black pudding boil, reduce the heat and let it simmer for about 25 minutes, turning constantly.

Cooking must go on for the time indicated to allow the blood to cook well, otherwise the taste would not be pleasant.

Off the heat, keep turning the cream until it is lukewarm and add to this the cinnamon sachet with the Rhum and half of the cedar and cocoa pieces. In a nice crystal bowl put the black pudding, garnish it with the pieces of the remaining cedar and cocoa, while around you will place the ladyfingers upright.

What could be more cheerful and tasty at Carnival than a dessert like this?

ALMOND FOAMS

Ingredients for 4 people

Almonds 5 oz - sugar 5 oz - 1 egg white

PREPARATION

Take them almonds and in a saucepan of boiling water, dip them and leave them for a few minutes.

Remove the almond skin that you will pass under the fresh water so that they remain very white.

The almonds will be dried and put in the oven at 200° F heat to lightly toast a light blond, while then they will have to be coarsely chopped like rice grains. In a bowl put the egg white and sugar and whisk with the electric whisk, occasionally putting a drop of lemon, as well as a grated lemon peel.

Continue working for at least 20 minutes until the mixture appears assembled and firm. Finally add the almonds.

With two teaspoons, take the mixture and place it on the buttered and floured oven plate; each biscuit must be the size of a small nut, spaced from each other.

Bake at a temperature of 325° F; you will see that the skimmers will widen and swell and the cooking will have to last for at least 20 minutes to complete.

Finally, they will appear slightly biscuit color, will be light, very delicate and will be eaten all in one breath.

SFOGLIATELLE FROLLE

Ingredients for 6 people

For the pasta: flour 20 oz - sugar 7 oz −3 egg yolks plus 1 whole egg - suet 7 oz - 1 pinch of salt

For the filling: 1 ½ cup of milk - semolina 4 oz - ricotta 7 oz - sugar 5 oz - 1 sachet of vanilla - ½ sachet of cinnamon - 2 tablespoons of orange water - candied fruit (cedar, cocoa, orange) 4 oz - 1 whole egg - 1 pinch of salt

PREPARATION

To prepare the dough, put the flour with all the ingredients on the table and mix everything together, work for 5 minutes until the pasta comes off the table and your hands.

If you have difficulty kneading you can add a glass of brandy or a few spoonfuls of milk.

Now let the dough rest and dedicate yourself to the filling.

Boil the milk and, while boiling, toss the semolina, sugar and a pinch of salt in one fell swoop.

Cook for 10 minutes, turning vigorously and without interruption.

Let the mixture cool and, at this point, add the ricotta that you have previously passed through a horsehair sieve, the beaten egg and all the other ingredients (the candied fruit must be cut into small pieces). Let's now go back to our panel which will have rested for an

173

hour; roll it out to a thickness of half a centimeter and with a glass of wine make many discs of even number.

Take two discs at a time and tie them to one end and, for each pair, put 1 spoonful of filling.

Turn one disc over onto the other and close the two edges with your wet fingers and give it a shell shape.

So you get about thirty puff pastries, brush them with egg yolk before spreading them on the buttered and floured oven plate.

Heat the oven to 400° F for the first 10 minutes thus reducing the temperature to 350° F. After another 10 minutes the sfogliatelle will be ready.

Given the capacity of the home ovens, the cooking will have to be done twice.

At the happy end of your business, pulverize your puff pastries with vanilla icing sugar.

SFOGLIATELLE RICCE

Ingredients for 6 people

For the pasta: flour 28 oz (possibly the American one) - water 5 oz - Lard 5 oz - 2 egg yolks - salt

For the filling: half a quart of milk - semolina 7 oz - hard cottage cheese 14 oz - sugar 8 oz - 1 sachet of vanilla - 2-3 drops of cinnamon - 3 tablespoons of orange water - candied fruit (cedar, cocoa, orange) 6 oz - 2 whole eggs - salt

PREPARATION

To prepare this type of sfogliatella, which is not difficult, you need to be familiar with the machine with which you make the tagliatelle (type of Italian pasta).

First of all, prepare the pasta by placing the flour on the table with cold water, a lard of suet, the 2 yolks and a pinch of salt.

Mix the dough well and work it first with the knuckles of your hands and then beating it with a rolling pin.

At this point divide the dough into various parts which will be kept divided in a nylon bag so that it does not dry out.

Each piece will be passed through the puff iron machine, going over the dough at least 3 times.

After all the pieces have run out, put them in one and put this piece in a nylon bag and let it rest for at least an hour.

After this time, divide the pasta into 6 equal parts and start the real processing. While the remaining suet (4 oz)

You will have liquefied over very low heat, having someone else help you, start passing the first piece of pasta from the machine from n ° 2 to n° 6 in order to obtain a very fine puff pastry.

As the dough comes out of this last pass, brush it by the person who helps you and wrapping it tightly on itself.

Once the first piece is finished, continue with the same procedure for the 2nd and then again for the 3rd, these last two pieces must be wrapped on the first roll.

At the end you will have a roll with a diameter of about 2.5 inch.

With the remaining 3 pieces use the same procedure in order to obtain another roll equal to the first.

Wrap both of them in plastic wrap and keep them in the refrigerator for 24 hours. The next day we think about the filling: boil the milk and, as soon as this raises the stamp, throw in the semolina, sugar, salt and, turning vigorously, cook for 15 minutes until you have obtained a firm dough but very smooth and without lumps.

Let the semolina cool down and then add the ricotta already passed in a horsehair sieve, the beaten eggs, vanilla, cinnamon, orange water and candied fruit cut into tiny pieces, completing the processing with a last vigorous stirring.

Let's go back to the pasta of the puff pastry: take the two rolls out of the refrigerator and cut them into 10 slices each of about 0.4 inch thus obtaining 20 slices.

Take each slice that will appear as a roll of tape and, starting from the center, lower the strips outwards, trying to thin the center of the slice in order to obtain a double shell that will serve to contain the filling you have already divided into 20 equal parts.

After introducing the attached filling or edges of the puff pastries with a drop of water.

In two batches bake the curls in the oven previously heated to 570° F and, after 10 minutes, decrease the heat to 475° F for another 10 minutes.

Your delicious puff pastries will be ready and it will be enough to sweeten them with vanilla icing. It was not easy to explain the whole process of this dessert, but follow my explanation as faithfully as possible and you will see that you will succeed.

For us, women of the South Italy, it is a point of pride to be able to make this typical dessert of our land, known all over the world.

STRUFFOLI

Ingredients for 10 people

For the pasta: flour 30 oz - 6 whole eggs - butter 2 oz - ½ small glass of anise - ½ small glass of Brandy - a pinch of salt

For the decoration: raw honey 20 oz - sugar 8 oz - the peel of 1 orange - pumpkin, candied citron and orange 3 oz - aniseed and cannellini beans 3 oz

PREPARATION

Flour the flour on the table, leaving some of it aside and in the center you will put the butter cut into small pieces, the anisette, the Brandy and a pinch of salt.

Begin to knead, putting one egg at a time and gradually absorb all the ingredients with the flour.

The dough should be a little softer than normal egg pasta and this due to the presence of butter and liqueurs.

Knead the dough for a good half hour, also beating it vigorously on the table, until it has assumed a soft and velvety appearance and, cutting the dough, you will not see that there will be small holes in this; put it to rest for about two hours covered and in a sheltered place.

After this time, divide the dough into small punches, but keep away the unused one that you will put in a plastic bag.

From these punches, first with your hands and then on the table, pull the sticks as big as the thin breadsticks and from these get the struffoli that must not be bigger than a chickpea.

After this phase we started frying. In a rather large pan with a triple bottom of stainless steel or cast iron and high sides, add plenty of oil, about three quarters of a liter, and bring the oil to medium heat.

Start frying by throwing, as a quantity, the bottom filled with struffoli of a fruit saucer.

They will be fried over medium heat but always at constant heat.

If the dough has been well worked you will see that the struffoli will swell filling the whole bottom of the pan.

Be careful because the oil during frying could create bubbles, for this the pan must have high edges and try to break them by continuing to turn with a wooden spoon.

After frying, in a 6-quarter pot, put honey, sugar and two fingers of water.

Melt all the mixture on the heat, always at moderate heat, and cook for about 10 minutes, until you see that a drop between your fingers will start to stick.

At this point, remove the pot from the heat and, little by little, put the struffoli with the peel of the fresh orange cut into very thin strips; mix gently to get the struffoli soaked in honey.

Arrange them on a round serving plate and, with wet hands, even a little pressing, you get a nice donut that you will garnish with candied fruit cut into small pieces, confetti and cannellini beans.

I think in Naples there is no happier dessert for this for a happy Christmas.

TARALLI OF "SUGARED NUNS"

Ingredients for 8 people

For the pasta: Flour 16 oz - sugar 4 oz - 4 tablespoons of seed oil - 3 whole eggs plus 1 yolk - ½ sachet of yeast - 1 grated lemon

For the cover: icing sugar 7 oz - 1 egg white - 2 sachets of vanilla - the juice of a ½ lemon

PREPARATION

If the eggs are large ones, weighing 3 oz each, the dose of the flour will be more than precise; instead if the eggs were of normal size, 2 oz, use a little less.

In a bowl or better in the mixer, put the whole eggs with the yolk and sugar and beat as much as possible, until a well swollen and frothy mixture is obtained; at this point you can alternately add the flour with the oil, a pinch of salt and the lemon grater.

The dough must be worked very hard, a good half hour, both by hand and with the whisk and must be soft as the dough of the bread and smooth as silk. Finally add the yeast and let this paste rest for half an hour.

Divide the dough into 20 equal pieces and form many rolls the size of a finger that you will join at the ends to obtain the taralli. Put 3 fingers of water in a wide and low pan with a diameter of 12 inch that you will boil on the fire.

Gently pour 3-4 taralli at a time and have them give a first stamp; with a shovel, remove the taralli from the base of the pan by turning them over, one more stamp and the taralli will surface.

Remove them with a slotted spoon and put them on a tea towel.

After this first cooking, place them on the oven plate, buttered and floured, and pass them in the preheated oven at a temperature of 350° F.

It will take 20 minutes to cook and you will see that your taralli will grow wonderfully almost reaching double the initial volume (they must practically peel off and this will happen both for the presence of the eggs and for the good processing).

Separately, whisk the egg whites until stiff and gradually add the icing sugar with vanilla and ½ lemon juice; you will get a thick cream, which you will spread with the brush on the taralli.

In a cool and airy place the icing will dry and the taralli will be ready for use; they will keep for many days, will have a very pleasant taste and a lot of substance.

TARTE WITH STRAWBERRIES

Ingredients for 8 people

For the pasta: flour 9 oz - butter 5 oz - 2 egg yolks - sugar 6 oz - milk a few tablespoons - ½ teaspoon salt

For the cover: strawberries 20 oz - raspberry or black currant jelly 10 oz - 4 spoons of sugar (2 of which for jelly and 2 for strawberries) - juice of 1 lemon

PREPARATION

Prepare the dough by placing the sifted flour on the table; in the center, put the softened butter cut into small pieces, the sugar, the salt and the two egg yolks with a few spoonfuls of milk.

Work the dough but not excessively, because it must be soft, and let it rest for at least an hour covered by a cloth in a sheltered place.

Then roll out the dough into a low tart pan about 11 inch in diameter.

After having buttered and floured it.

Regarding this operation, to obtain that the dough does not break, first lay it on a sheet of wax paper on which you have previously sprinkled some flour; turning the sheet of paper with the dough stretched out, you will see that the sheet of pastry will lay down in the pan without breaking.

At this point, tap the dough with a fork and cover it with aluminum foil, lay a layer of dry beans on top of it, which will prevent the pasta from rising during cooking. Bake now at 350° F for about 25 minutes.

Remove the tarte from the oven to free it from the aluminum foil and the beans and put it back in the oven for another 10 minutes to make it take on the color. I advise you to keep the beans in a jar, to use them some other time in other tartes.

For the decoration, take the strawberries and wash them with white wine (they would lose flavor with the water) and then cut them in half and season with the sugar and lemon, leaving them to flavor for a while in this sauce. Remove them, drain them with much grace, and cover the base of the tarte completely.

Separately, dissolve the gelatin in a saucepan with 2 tablespoons of water and 2 tablespoons of sugar over low heat; as Soon as the gelatin is dissolved, spread it warm on the strawberries which will take on a bright appearance, helping to give the cake a magnificent effect. Coating of the tarte should be performed no later than 1 hour before serving to prevent it from losing its consistency.

This dessert can be accompanied by fresh whipped cream and served separately in an elegant tray.

It is mandatory that the tare with strawberries is served by the landlady, because it is she who must receive the sure applause.

TARTE AI MARRONI

Ingredients for 8 people

For the pasta: flour 12 oz - butter 2 oz - margarine or lard 2 oz - sugar 5 oz - 3 egg yolks - 1 drop of milk - grated ½ lemon - salt

For the filling: chestnuts 20 oz - cocoa 2 oz - sugar 6 oz - butter 2 oz - 3 whole eggs - half a sachet of vanilla - pumpkin and candied citron 2 oz - ½ glass of milk

PREPARATION

Prepare the shortcrust pastry by placing the sprinkle flour, sliced butter, lard or margarine, sugar, egg yolks, a pinch of salt and a dash of milk on the table.

Knead quickly and you will see that soon the dough will come off your hands and the table.

Put the dough together and put it in a cool and sheltered place, covered with a cloth to let it rest for at least two hours.

For the filling, peel the chestnuts but leave the skin on and, covered with water and a pinch of salt, cook over low heat.

As soon as they are cooked, peel them and pass them through a horsehair sieve. To the chestnut puree add the cocoa that you have melted with the sugar and butter in half a glass of milk.

Turn the mixture well until a thick and homogeneous cream is obtained.

In a baking pan 11 inch in diameter and 0.8 inch high, buttered and floured, spread just over half the dough.

To the chestnut cream add the 3 beaten eggs and make sure that, while turning, the mixture absorbs all the eggs, while at the end you will only have to add the cinnamon, pumpkin and cedar.

The cream will be ready to be poured on the shortcrust pastry. With the remaining pasta you will make a nice reticulated with 0.4 inch wide strips and cut with the wheel to cut the pasta.

Close the surplus of the dough at the edges and join it with the round tip of a small knife. Brush the surface of the cake with an egg red and bake.

The cooking must go on for 50 minutes or a little more at a temperature of 350° F. This dessert is also delicious and is more than suitable to offer it at a party for young people.

I recommend you prepare the dessert the day before use in order to best blend the flavors.

TARTE TATIN

Ingredients for 6 people

3 whole eggs - sugar 6 oz - flour 3 oz - scented apples 16 oz - milk cream 14 oz - 2 sachets of vanilla - sugar for caramel 5 oz

PREPARATION

Take a round shape with a capacity of 1 quart, with a diameter of 8 inch and a height of 2.8 inch, put in it the sugar for the caramel and, over low heat, let it caramelize in a blond color.

Move the form so that the hot caramel is uniformly deposits up to cover the entire inner wall.

On the caramel, still hot, arrange pressing, next to each other the slices of apple cut into not too thin wedges.

Sprinkle the two sachets of vanilla on the apples mixed with two tablespoons of icing sugar.

Apart with the whisk, at a reduced speed, whip the egg yolks with the sugar until you get a frothy cream; add, little by little, the sifted flour and 4 spoons of cream.

Finally add gently to the egg whites until stiff and cover the apples with this mixture.

Put in a preheated oven at a temperature of 350° F for 45 minutes. The cake will grow beautifully; turn it warm and you will see that it will look splendid with its beautiful caramelized apples at the top.

Serve the cake accompanied by the unsweetened cream in a gravy boat.

It is a typical dessert of French cuisine created by Mr. Tatin, but it is worth adding it to the range of our desserts. Seeing is believing!

YOGURT CAKE

Ingredients for 6 people

1 jar of whole yogurt - 3 jars of flour yogurt - 2 jars of sugar yogurt - 1 jar of sunflower oil yogurt - 3 whole eggs - the scraping of 1 lemon - 2 teaspoons of baking powder

PREPARATION

In a large bowl put the yogurt; take the empty jar, wash it, dry it and use it to measure the ingredients (flour, sugar, oil).

Add the egg yolks and set aside the egg whites in another bowl.

Mix the dough and work it with the electric whisk for about 15 minutes until you have obtained a thick but light and frothy cream.

Separately whip the egg whites until stiff adding gently, little by little, to the dough after adding the yeast.

Take a shape with a hole of 9 inch in diameter and 2.8 inch in height and, after having greased and floured it, pour the ready-made mixture. You just have to bake the cake having previously heated the oven.

The temperature, during cooking, must be 350° F and will last for 50 minutes.

To confirm that the cake is cooked, simply insert a knitting needle into the cake which must come out clean.

This foresight applies to all desserts as each oven has different characteristics, so both the temperature and the cooking duration that I give is indicative, it can vary from oven to oven.

Our dessert during cooking will grow splendidly and will have a magnificent appearance when baked.

With these doses you will have a light and appetizing cake that will have the characteristics, due to the presence of yogurt, to keep fresh for a few days as long as you have the foresight to keep it in a cellophane bag, provided that the kids do not eat it immediately.

This dessert will be very suitable for breakfast in the morning or for a snack for the kids or for tea with friends.

ALMOND CAKE

Ingredients for 8 people

Shelled almonds 10 oz - sugar 7 oz - 6 fresh eggs - 1 glass of Strega liqueur - 2 tablespoons of potato starch - ½ packet of baking powder - orange peel 1 oz - 2 teaspoons of bitter almond extract

PREPARATION

This cake is very tasty, if it is performed with precision it will give you a lot of satisfaction.

The execution is simple.

Take the almonds and, in a medium-sized saucepan, give them a light boil and then immediately throw them in fresh water so they can remain very white.

Free them from their skin and over very low heat let them dry in the oven.

Take the grinder and grind the almonds one grit at a time, which must have the grain of the ground coffee.

Separately divide the eggs, the red ones from the whites, and put them in two bowls making sure that the whites do not go the slightest trace of the reds that hinder their whipping.

Add the sugar to the reds and whisk them for at least 30 minutes with the electric whisk until the mixture is clear and frothy and goes down into the cup in a ribbon. Add the almond flour, baking powder, starch, glass of Strega to the mixture and, if the dough is too hard, you can add a few spoonfuls of milk (it must be like a thick cream).

Finally, add the extract of bitter and white almonds whisked until stiff with the electric whisk, adding them to the mixture a little at a time by gently moving the wooden spoon from the bottom up and not in a circular direction.

In a baking pan with a diameter of 11 inch and 2.8 inch high, buttered and floured, put the mixture and bake at a temperature of 350°F.

The cooking must last for 50 minutes and will be completed when introducing a knitting needle into the cake will come out clean.

A little tip: do not open the oven during cooking.

Once cooked the cake will be covered with powdered sugar.

Note: if you have difficulty finding the bitter almond extract you can replace it by adding some bitter almonds to the almonds, otherwise you will eliminate this ingredient. The dessert will not have a bitterness which is ultimately its characteristic, but ... patience.

BROWN ALMOND CAKE

Ingredients for 8 people

Sugar 8 oz - butter 8 oz - dark chocolate 4 oz - 5 whole eggs - almonds ground with the peel 8 oz - 3 tablespoons of potato starch - ½ sachet of baking powder - 1 small glass of rum.

PREPARATION

In a rather large bowl put the butter, which you will have kept at room temperature, and with the sugar mix it with the whisk until it becomes white and frothy.

Divide the egg yolks from the whites and with a teaspoon gradually put the yolks in the processed butter cream; but do not put the teaspoon of red if the cream has not completely absorbed the previous one.

Separately, with the coffee grinder well cleaned, grind the almonds with all their peel (clean them first with a cloth); the grain must be like that of coffee, but do not overdo it otherwise the almonds will chase the oil and the dessert will not be light. Meanwhile, put the chocolate in the oven, at very moderate heat, to which, once softened, you can add the small glass of rum.

After the egg yolks, add the chocolate with the rum, the almond powder, the potato starch and the half sachet of yeast to the mixture. Beat the egg whites until stiff and gently add them to the dough a little at a time. In a baking pan with a diameter of 10 inch,

3 inch high, buttered and floured, pour the prepared cream and bake at a temperature of 350° F for 45 minutes.

After this time the cake will grow and will be well cooked if by introducing a knitting needle it will come out clean. Let the cake cool down and turn it out by covering it with plenty of vanilla icing sugar.

Ultimately this should be the famous and delicious Caprese cake... keep the secret.....

RICOTTA CAKE

Ingredients for 10 people

For the pasta: flour 14 oz - butter 6 oz - sugar 6 oz - 1 whole egg - 1 lemon grater - ½ brandy shell - salt to taste

For the filling: ricotta 20 oz - 3 whole eggs plus 1 yolk - sugar 10 oz - 1 sachet of cream 7 oz - 3 curls of fresh orange peel - ground almonds 4 oz - ½ bottle of bitter almonds

PREPARATION

First prepare the pasta by placing the flour on the table with all the ingredients and working it a little until it is detached from the table and from your hands, which will happen in a short time.

Leave the dough to rest for about an hour in a cool, sheltered place covered with a napkin.

In the meantime, prepare the stuffing and, first of all, immerse the almonds in a saucepan with boiling water, leave them for a few minutes while then you will pass them under fresh water so that they remain white and free them from their skin.

Pass them in the oven, after drying them, at a moderate temperature (200°F) so that they can completely lose humidity, then pass them through the chopper to get a powder. Pass the ricotta from a horsehair sieve and add the eggs plus the yolk beaten with the crepe, the sugar, the almond powder, the cream, the orange cut into very thin pieces, as well as the bitter almond extract.

In a pan 12 inch in diameter and 0.8 inch high or slightly more, buttered and floured, spread a little more than half of the dough, with a thin sheet and, on this, pour the padding.

With the rest of the dough, which will also go to this stretch, you get ribbons to complete the cake with the wheel, placing them on a wire rack.

Fold the edges and strip them with a round-tipped knife. Bake and let your cake cook for an hour and a half at a moderate temperature (300° F).

Let the cake cool, turn it out and sprinkle it with vanilla icing sugar.

It is a dessert with a delicate flavor that is worth preparing in order to be counted among the best you have made.

APPLE PIE

Ingredients for 8 people

Flour 6 oz - 2 eggs - sugar 6 oz - margarine 1 oz - butter 1 oz - 1 glass of milk - the grated peel of 1 lemon - 1 sachet of vanilla - 1 sachet of baking powder - apples 20 oz - macaroons 2 oz

PREPARATION

Peel the apples and cut them into thin wedges, set them aside. In the meantime, beat the butter, margarine and sugar in a bowl.

You can initially mix the fats with the sugar using your hands and then continue with a wooden spoon until you have obtained a frothy cream.

Add the egg yolks one at a time to the mixture and, subsequently, the flour sifted with the yeast, the milk, a little at a time, while finally add the vanilla and the grated lemon.

Separately whip the egg whites that you will put into the mixture gently and you will have completed the processing.

In a 9.5 inch diameter and 2.8 inch high pan, buttered and floured, pour the mixture and, on this, arrange the apples starting from the outside of the pan in concentric circles and placing the wedges not on the side but vertically on the longer side.

At the end you will have the cake prone and it will look like a beautiful rose: finally crumble the _amaretti_ (type of Italian biscuit) on this with a sprinkle of sugar and bake at 350° F for about an hour.

This dessert, basically easy to perform, will not disappoint you and will be the joy of your children.

MERINGUE CAKE WITH STRAWBERRIES

Ingredients for 10 people

8 egg whites - sugar 20 oz - the grated peel of 2 lemons - sweet whipped cream 20 oz - strawberries 20 oz

PREPARATION

Whip the egg whites until stiff and add all the sugar, one teaspoon at a time, continuing without interruption to whip the whites.

This operation will last more than an hour because the secret of the success of the meringue is that the sugar is perfectly absorbed and dissolved in the egg whites. In two low trays with a diameter of 11 inch, place two well-buttered aluminum sheets inside and pour the mixture equally, sprinkling the grated lemon on both. Bake the two trays on the two floors of the oven at low temperature, about 200° F. The two meringues, rather than cooking, will have to dry out. This operation will last about an hour and a half; you will find that they are ready because they will detach from the edges and appear solidified. At this point the game is done, you just have to pack the cake. Prepare separately and strawberries washed in white wine, drain and sprinkle them with sugar (3 tablespoons) and squeeze half a lemon over them. On a serving plate, put a disc of meringue and arrange half of the cream with half of the strawberries; cover with the other meringue disk and, on top and sideways, spread the remaining cream appearing it with a long blade knife. Finally, artistically arrange the remaining strawberries to crown. And ... enjoy your meal.

CARNIVAL TORTELLI

Ingredients for 6 people

Flour 8 oz - butter 4 oz - ¼ quart of water - 6 eggs - 1 tablespoon of sugar - 1 pinch of salt - icing vanilla sugar 4 oz

PREPARATION

Boil the water with the butter, salt and sugar; after boiling, throw the flour all at once and turn vigorously, cook for 10 minutes on moderate heat; you will hear the pasta sizzle in the pan.

Transport the dough in a well-capable and solid bowl and let it cool.

At this point start to incorporate the first egg and do not put the next one if the pasta has not completely absorbed the previous one; the overall process will last about 30 minutes.

Let the dough rest for 2 hours in a covered and well-sheltered place.

Put a pan on the fire with plenty of oil and wait until it has not reached an excessive heat.

Meanwhile, take a teaspoon and make small nuts from the dough that you will gradually throw in the pan.

The tortelli will swell and double in volume; once cooked pass them on paper towels, put them on a serving plate and sprinkle them with plenty of vanilla icing sugar.

In a Carnival meeting these tortelli will be a worthy completion to the more than traditional SANGUINACCIO.

STUFFED CHESTNUT TRUNK

Ingredients for 8 people

For the basic pasta: chestnuts 40 oz - sugar 6 oz - dark chocolate 4 oz - butter 2 oz -1 glass of Rhum - 1 sachet of vanilla

For the filling: butter 6 oz - sugar 5 oz - 2 egg yolks - 1 cup of coffee - chopped chocolate 2 oz

PREPARATION

Take the chestnuts and, after having freed them from their brown skin, put them to cook in plenty of lightly salted water.

As soon as the chestnuts are cooked, remove the other peel and pass them through a horsehair sieve, massing them occasionally with your hands.

In a large saucepan put the chestnut puree, sugar, dark chocolate softened in the oven at moderate heat, butter, Rhum.

Turn vigorously to obtain a thick paste and then let it cool.

Meanwhile, prepare the mixture to fill by placing the butter and sugar in a bowl; work the mixture also with the electric whisk until you have obtained a creamy and frothy cream; only then can you add the egg yolks, one teaspoon at a time, not putting the next one if the cream has not absorbed the previous one.

With the same system then add the coffee.

Finally you will have a beautiful cream that will be greatly increased in volume. Meanwhile, take a rather large, wet and wrung out tea towel, put it on the table and spread the chestnuts mixture with your wet hands.

Fold the 4 sides of the dishtowel on this and lay with your hands until you get a uniform chestnut rectangle, about 0.6 inch thick and with sides 10 x 12. You will only have to spread evenly more than half of the ready-made cream and, helping yourself with the edges of the cloth, wrap the chestnut mixture on itself with the cream.

Gently put the cake on the serving plate, garnish it with the remaining cream and make grooves, like a tree trunk, with a sweet comb or with a fork.

Complete the garnish with chocolate chips, refrigerate for a few hours and then serve. It is a dessert that is prepared in the autumn at the time of chestnuts and, in addition to having an inviting appearance, it is delicious.

"ZEPPOLE A BIGNET DI SAN GIUSEPPE"

Ingredients for 8 people

For the pasta: flour 9 oz - 6 eggs - butter 5 oz - water 10 oz - 1 pinch of salt.

For the garnish / cream: milk 20 oz - 3 egg yolks - flour 2 oz - sugar 4 oz - black cherry jam 4 oz - 1 sachet of vanilla.

PREPARATION

The ideal for baking the dough is the clean wrist which is that typical copper pan for pastry chefs, with round walls with a long handle; if you haven't, use a high-walled pan.

Add the water with the butter and salt; as soon as it boils, remove the pan from the heat and throw the flour all at once.

Put back on the heat and turn vigorously by cooking the dough for 6-7 minutes, until it begins to sizzle.

Pour the dough into a bowl and as soon as it is warm, start pouring the first egg, working well for at least 6-7 minutes.

Switch to the second egg always with 6-7 minutes of processing, and repeat the operation for all the eggs.

Taking care each time to make each egg absorb well to the mixture. It will be preferable to prepare this pasta a few hours earlier so that it rests and is more elastic. With a syringe for sweets, with a wide mouth, place the zeppole on the oven plate, eight at a time, spaced 0.8 inch apart, making the syringe a double turn, the second superimposed on the first.

Then in the preheated oven bake at a temperature of 425° F.

When, after 10 minutes, you have seen that the zeppole have swollen and just colored, decrease the heat to 350° F and leave it in the oven for 10 minutes. With these quantities will come 16 zeppole, then proceed with the second batch. There is no need to grease the pasta as the zeppole will come off on their own, simply moisten it.

For the garnish: beat the three egg yolks with the sugar, add the milk, in which you will have diluted the flour cold, passing it through a colander. Put on the heat at medium temperature, adding a lemon peel to the mixture; the cream will always be turned in the same direction and you will see that after about 10 minutes it will have taken on the right consistency.

Let the cream cool down after adding the vanilla packet.

Sprinkle the zeppole with vanilla icing sugar; with the syringe with the smaller mouth make the top of each zeppola a nice curl of cream, and complete the garnish with 2-3 black cherries.

These zeppole can also be fried, but the processing will be more delicate; in this case prepare 16 squares of greaseproof paper of 10 inch each side and on each one, after having greased it, place the zeppola.

At the beginning the oil must have moderate heat then, as soon as the zeppola has deflated, increase the heat.

Lift the zeppola from the oil together with the paper that you can easily detach. Continue also with these zeppole to the garnish.

"ZEPPOLE A KRAFFEN"

Ingredients for 8 people

Flour 20 oz - butter 2 oz - 6 egg yolks - 1 stick of yeast 1 oz - 2 medium sized potatoes 12 oz - grated lemon - half egg shell of cognac.

For the garnish: sugar 6 oz - 1 sachet of cinnamon.

PREPARATION

Sprinkle the sifted flour on the table, in the center of this the potatoes cooked and mashed with the potato passer, then the other ingredients: the egg yolks, the butter cut into slices, the yeast, the grated lemon, the half shell of cognac egg and salt enough.

Knead the dough until it is well blended, no more than 6-7 minutes since the potatoes would tend with too much processing to bring out the water.

Grow the dough in a bowl for about 2 and a half hours, until the volume has doubled. At this point divide the dough into many equally sized punches, and from each of these pull a 12 inch long torch, bigger in the center, with the thin tips that will be superimposed and crushed with your finger to avoid opening the wedges frying.

Arrange the zeppole on a well floured table and cover them with a cloth, leaving them to rise for another half hour.

Now in a pan with high sides, with plenty of medium heat oil, fry the zeppole two at a time, pull them up gradually with a fork making them well drain.

You will have a plate ready to which you will have mixed the cinnamon with the sugar, and in this sugar give each zeppola a turn and a turn.

You can put them on the dish. I advise you to consume the zeppole no later than two hours from its packaging.

They are more fragrant and so tasty that you will have the pleasure and joy of making them many times.

"ZUPPA INGLESE"

Ingredients for 8 people

Sponge cake: 5 eggs - 5 tablespoons of flour mixed with potato starch - 5 tablespoons of sugar - 1 tip of baking powder

For the filling: cream - ¾ of milk - 6 egg yolks - starch 3 oz - sugar 6 oz - 1 sachet of vanilla - 1 lemon peel - cocoa 2 oz - apricot or black cherry or blackberry jam 6 oz

For the syrup: 1 glass of water - sugar 5 oz - 1 lemon peel - 1 orange peel - 1 small glass of rum - 1 small glass of Strega liqueur

For the meringue: 3 egg whites - sugar 6 oz

PREPARATION

Prepare the sponge cake as per the recipe in this book but using a rectangular baking tray measuring 12 x 10 inch.

Aside from the prepared cream: beat the egg yolks with the sugar until they are well whipped and come down from the spoon in a ribbon, dissolve the starch in a little cold milk, add all the milk and, through a strainer, pour it onto the eggs.

Pour the whole mixture with a lemon peel and vanilla, bring almost to a boil and always turn from one direction only.

After 10 minutes of cooking the cream will be ready, take a part of it and stirring on the fire for a few minutes, add the cocoa until it is absorbed by the cream. Prepare the syrup with water and sugar, boil it for 6-7 minutes. Finally, add the Rhum and the Strega liqueur out of the heat. Cut the sponge cake into 0.4 inch long slices and cover the bottom of a baking dish (12 inch long by 9 inch) with the syrup, now cold, then place the yellow cream and the jam in piles.

Make another sponge cake soil, wet this too, arrange the cream, the chocolate, as well as the jam, cover everything with the remaining slices of sponge cake which will also go wet.

Prepare the meringue by beating the whites until stiff steaks and adding the sugar, little by little.

With a syringe for sweets with a rather wide mouth, make many strips next to each other, to cover the entire surface.

Bake for about 10 minutes at 350° F and, as soon as the meringue has become a little colored, take it out.

Let the English soup rest for at least 24 hours in the refrigerator, you will eat something really delicious.

ICE CREAM – SEMIFREDDI

COFFEE ICE CREAM WITH CREAM

Ingredients for 6 people

¼ quart of milk - coffee ½ cup - sugar 6 oz - 4 egg yolks

PREPARATION

First of all, prepare a machine with three cups of strong coffee (the quantity should correspond to the marked ingredients).

Work the egg yolks with the sugar, as for the cream ice cream, pour the milk already boiled with the coffee and a pinch of salt, turn the mixture well then put it in the container where you have boiled the milk to boil it for about 10 minutes. Once the cream has cooled, put it in the ice cream maker in the freezer.

After 45 minutes the ice cream will be ready, pour it into a tray and leave it in the freezer for another 15 minutes.

You can serve ice cream in the cups garnishing everything with tufts of whipped cream. For this quantity just a sachet of whipping cream from 7 oz.

The composition of this ice cream is also worthy of much consideration.

CHOCOLATE ICE CREAM

Ingredients

Half a quart of milk - sugar 7 oz - 4 egg yolks - dark chocolate 2 oz

PREPARATION

Boil the milk with the fondant until it has completely melted. Separately, beat the egg yolks with the sugar to obtain a thick, frothy and light cream.

Add the milk with the chocolate, also hot; bring to a boil.

Let the cream cool and pass it in the ice cream maker in the freezer for 45 minutes.

You can serve in cups with a sprig of cream.

The kids will go crazy.

ORANGE ICE CREAM

Ingredients for 6 people

Juice of 4 oranges (1 cup of liquid) - the juice of 1 lemon - the grated peel of 2 oranges - sugar 8 oz - water 1 cup - 1 egg white - 1 small glass of liqueur (Gran Marnier or Curacao)

PREPARATION

Of the 4 oranges, grate the peel of two.

Squeeze the juice of the 4 oranges which should correspond to 1 cup of liquid equal to a glass of water.

Add to this juice also 1 squeezed lemon and the grated 2 oranges. Aside, boil the water with the sugar for a few minutes, so that it dissolves.

As soon as the syrup has cooled, add it to the prepared juice. Beat an egg white by adding it last to the mixture that you will pour into the ice cream pan with a capacity of 1 quart, already left to cool in the freezer 30 minutes before.

Processing in the freezer will continue for about 45 minutes; at this point, remove the ice cream maker from the freezer, add the liqueur and stir to mix everything. Put the pan back in the freezer for another 30 minutes so that the ice cream can harden again.

The presence of egg white will make the ice cream pasty and well whipped. Once upon a time there was a sorbet shop for ice creams, then wooden tubs with an iron box were used and the work was manual and very tiring.

Now with electric ice cream parlors, which can be placed in our freezer, ice cream is within everyone's reach.

For a more pleasant appearance, you can put the ice cream in the skins of 6 medium-sized oranges to which you have cut a lid at the top and empty their fruit, taking care not to break the skin.

This ice cream is excellent both in winter and in summer for a late lunch and will be 100% natural.

HAZELNUT ICE CREAM

Ingredients

Hazelnuts 4 oz - half a quart of milk - sugar 6 oz - 3 egg yolks

Homemade ice creams are a real delicacy, even if they will be packed by you in the winter, your children will love them enormously.

PREPARATION

Toast the hazelnuts of a nice blond and remove the skin, pound them in the mortar little by little, and add a few drops of milk to obtain a thick paste.

When the operation is complete, put the milk to boil and in this introduce the hazelnut paste by boiling for a few minutes.

Let the milk cool with the hazelnuts and pass it for the sieve.

Separately beat the egg yolks with the sugar and as soon as you have obtained a thick but light cream that will come down from the bowl in strips, add the cold milk mixture with the hazelnuts little by little.

Put back on the fire and bring almost to a boil. Leave to cool again and pass through the ice cream maker.

After 45 minutes the ice cream will be ready to be served.

CREAM ICE CREAM

Ingredients for 6 people

Half a quart of milk - 4 egg yolks - sugar 6 oz - the peel of 1 lemon - 2 sachets of sugar - 1 pinch of salt

PREPARATION

Beat the egg yolks with the sugar in a bowl until they become frothy and the mixture, lifted with a wooden spoon, will not drop into the bowl in a ribbon. Separately, boil the milk with the lemon zest and a pinch of salt and, hot, it will be poured on the egg mixture already worked.

Turn evenly and pour everything into the milk jug where you first boiled the milk (for creams in general the milk jug with a rather narrow bottom is fine).

Simmer the mixture for about 10 minutes but, be careful, that the fire is very slow otherwise the eggs would tear. Let the cream cool down and put it in the ice cream maker tray, previously cooled in the freezer.

Put the ice cream in the freezer and let the ice cream maker go for 45 minutes, the ice cream maker's spatulas will stop, take it out of the freezer and put the ice cream in the single tray that you will put again in the freezer for 15 minutes to freeze.

Put the cream in the cups and, for a touch of class, pour a spoonful of whiskey on each cup. Good ice cream!

The husbands will console themselves.

HAZELNUT PARFAIT

Ingredients for 6 people

5 whole eggs minus 1 egg white - sugar 12 oz - water 10 oz - hazelnuts 4 oz - whipped cream 16 oz or 2 bags of whipping cream

PREPARATION

Put the hazelnuts in the oven at a moderate temperature (270° F) to toast them lightly: with the grater remove the cutlets, crush them in the mortar adding a few spoonfuls of water (part of the ingredients) until you get a thick paste.

Boil the remaining water and pour in the hazelnut paste, add a few more stamps and leave to cool, then pass the mixture through a sieve.

Separately, whip the reds with the sugar, add the hazelnut mixture to them and, in a water bath, put everything, better in a small dish, on the fire to beat it with a hand whisk.

The cream will condense and increase in volume, but be careful the water in the water bath will quiver but not boil.

Off the heat, continue to turn gently and, as soon as the mixture has cooled, gently add first the egg whites until stiff and then the whipped cream.

You just have to put the parfait in a plum-cake shape about 10 inch long, covering it with an aluminum sheet that must come out from the shape of a few centimeters, and then put it in the freezer for 12 hours. you will see that the result of this hazelnut parfait will be excellent.

CHOCOLATE SEMIFREDDO

Ingredients for 10 people

4 whole eggs - sugar 6 oz - dark chocolate 4 oz - whipped cream 16 oz - chopped chocolate 4 oz

PREPARATION

If you have an electric whisk, the process will be much faster.

In a capable bowl put the egg yolks with the sugar and work this mixture until you see that the eggs will be well whipped and will come down to a ribbon.

With the whisk it will take 10 minutes while with the wooden spoon it will take at least 20 minutes.

Separately you will have melted the dark chocolate in a bain-marie or in a low temperature oven. When the chocolate has melted, add it lukewarm to the beaten eggs.

Separately, beat the whites until stiff and put them in the mixture after pouring the cream in them, being careful to pour these 2 ingredients little by little and gently with a movement of the spoon, not circular but from the outside towards the center of the bowl, until the whole compound is not well blended.

Now take a shape (the one used for plum-cakes), about 11 inch long by covering it with an aluminum sheet that must come out from the shape of a few centimeters; pour the mixture and put it in the freezer for 12 hours.

When you need to serve the dessert, take it out of the freezer and remove it from the shape by pulling the edges of the aluminum foil.

The semifreddo turned inside the serving dish will be easily freed from the aluminum foil; garnish it with chocolate chips. When serving, you can cut the semifreddo with a knife, with a wet blade, into slices of about 1 centimeter.

This tasty dessert will be enough for 10 people and its authenticity will be the best you can offer.

SPIRITS

CEDRINO

Ingredients

135 leaves of lemon grass - alcohol at 95° 1 quart - water 24 oz - sugar 26 oz

PREPARATION

Take the fresh and fragrant lemon grass leaves, choose them one by one, clean them with a clean cloth without being creased, immerse them in alcohol and leave them to infuse for 40 days in the dark.

Prepare the syrup, boiling the water with the sugar for about 10 minutes.

When the syrup has cooled, mix it with the alcohol that you have freed from the leaves.

Filter the liqueur through filter paper or cotton wool and let it age for at least 6 months.

You will have an excellent liqueur which will also be an excellent digestive.

MANDARIN LIQUEUR

Ingredients

Alcohol at 95° 1 quart - ½ quart of water - sugar 20 oz - 1 handful of confetti 12 fresh medium - sized thin-skinned mandarins

PREPARATION

Remove the peels from the mandarins, taking care to obtain only the peel and not the bread (the white part); also do this operation with great delicacy and attention without rubbing them so as not to spill the ether contained in it, the latter will give the flavor to the liqueur.

Put the alcohol in a large jar with a lid, add the tangerine peels, confetti and cap. Let this infusion mature for 12 days without forgetting to shake it every day at least once.

On the 12th day, prepare the syrup by boiling the water with the sugar for about ten minutes, let it cool and mix it with the alcohol to which you will have removed the peel of the mandarins and the confetti. Pass the liqueur in the bottles filtering it with filter paper or cotton wool. With this quantity will come 2 bottles of 1 liter; let the liqueur mature for 1 year.

After time, your liqueur will be clear as a crystal and a real nectar. You will be proud of it.

NOCILLO

Ingredients

30 fresh walnuts with their peel - alcohol at 95° 1,5 quart - cinnamon 0.1 oz - 5 cloves - china peel 2 oz - 2 curls of lemon zest - 2 nutmegs

For the syrup: half a quart of water - sugar 30 oz

PREPARATION

An ancient custom says that this magnificent liqueur should be prepared on St. John's day.

Ultimately, only at the end of June the walnuts will be at the right point for this preparation.

Cut the walnuts into 4 wedges (they will be soft and easily cut), place them in a large jar with the stopper together with the alcohol and spices. Leave them to infuse for 40 days, you will have to shake the pot every day and keep it in the natural light of a well-lit environment.

After this time, with a colander, pass the alcohol which will have taken on a brown color.

Aside, boil the water with the sugar for 10 minutes, allow the syrup to cool and mix it with the ready-made alcohol. Transfer the liqueur into the bottles (about 2 and a half liters will come) filtering it with filter paper or cotton wool.

As you well know, the nocillo (*or nocino*) is, among the homemade liqueurs, perhaps the best and, you can serve it with real pleasure in the Christmas holidays, having to rest at least six months.

NOCILLO (in another way)

Ingredients

30 already used for the 1st nocillo - dry white wine of excellent quality quart 2 - sugar 8 oz - water 1 cup

PREPARATION

When you have completed the 1st nocillo, you are advised not to throw away the walnuts used at the time and prepare the 2nd nocillo which will be an excellent aperitif to have at home.

Take the walnuts, dip them in the white wine and leave them to infuse for 48 hours.

After the necessary time, prepare the syrup with water and sugar by boiling it for 6-7 minutes.

Remove the walnuts from the wine, mix the syrup with it and filter it in the bottles with a funnel to which you will have placed either filter paper or cotton wool.

VARIOUS RECIPES

BECHAMEL

Ingredients

¼ quart of milk - 2 tablespoons of flour - butter 1 oz - salt to taste

PREPARATION

Aside, boil the milk. In a small pan, melt the butter and add the flour which you will let toast for a few minutes; then pour the hot milk a little at a time, turning vigorously until a thick and velvety cream is obtained.

Pour the béchamel on the table, spread it out, let it cool and cut it into squares. The table should be wet.

POTATO CROQUETTES

Ingredients for 6 people

Yellow potatoes hard paste 60 oz - 3 eggs - parmesan 3 oz - breadcrumbs 6 oz

PREPARATION

First of all cook the potatoes well covered in water but without a lid.

Once the peeled potatoes are cooked and pass them through the dough, on this occasion it would be better, for an excellent result, the marble mortar since the boiled potatoes would spin.

In a salad bowl, where you have already put the mashed potatoes, add the butter, parmesan and three eggs minus an egg white which will be used to pack the croquettes.

Work the dough energetically and well. You can prepare the croquettes with wet hands; passed the beaten egg white on each of these and finally roll them in the breadcrumbs.

Do everything very gently being a soft paste. In a pan with hot oil, fry the croquettes 3 at a time, no more, one turn and one turn will make them blond and crisp.

To your taste, inside each croquette, you can put a provola nut and you will have the OPTIMUM.

SPLEEN CROUTONS

Ingredients for 8 people

Veal spleen 5 oz - 3 chicken livers - butter 2 oz - 3 tablespoons of olive oil - ½ onion - 1 celery rib - 1 carrot - 2 salted anchovies - 1 tablespoon of breadcrumbs - ½ glass of dry _marsala_ (type of Italian wine) - 2 loaves of French bread - butter for garnish 2 oz

PREPARATION

Put the onion in a small pan with a well-chopped celery and carrot, a finger of glass of water and, over low heat, let the vegetables soften until the water has completely evaporated; add the butter, oil and, always on low heat, let the vegetables brown.

Aside, since the spleen will have its skin, with a knife open it horizontally and scratch all its substance.

A thick red cream will come out. Add the spleen pulp, the livers (the tender part) to the well browned beaten and cook gently for about 15 minutes, cooking the sauce with the marsala.

Finally, add the cleaned, washed and chopped anchovies and add a few more stamps to the sauce with the addition of a little breadcrumbs. As soon as the mixture has cooled, pass it through the chopper to get a thick cream.

Cut the whips of bread into slices and, on these, spread the spleen cream. On top of each slice, as a final touch, put a little bow of butter in the center.

It is a Tuscan specialty that was once found in the stalls of the bini and the ladies, during their shopping, went to enjoy with joy "the crostino with the spleen".

This specialty may well be included in the best appetizers and is always presented by all the Tuscans at Christmas and Easter lunches.

TRADITIONAL MAYONNAISE

Ingredients

1 egg red - sunflower oil 1 cup (equal to a glass of water) - 1 pinch of salt - the juice of ½ lemon

PREPARATION

The ideal would be to mount this type of mayonnaise in the marble mortar (the cold walls facilitate the processing) but, in the absence of this, take a bowl with thick walls and introduce the egg red.

Start the process by always turning from the same direction with a wooden spoon and not a metal one, without adding oil.

After a few minutes, so that the mayonnaise does not go crazy, put the oil in a drop while after completing the processing with a greater quantity of oil (a little spoonful at a time) and do not add more if the sauce has not absorbed the one already put.

Finally, dilute the mixture with the lemon juice in which you have dissolved the salt.

This sauce is also excellent and some like it more than the previous one.

RAPID EXECUTION MAYONNAISE

Ingredients for 4 people

1 whole egg - sunflower oil 1 cup (equal to a glass of water) - plus 2 more spoons of the said oil - ½ squeezed lemon - salt to taste

PREPARATION

Put the whole egg in the blender, the two spoons of oil, the juice of half a lemon, a pinch of salt and give a few strokes with the blender to get the ingredients to mix well. Put the blender back into operation by pouring the two deciliters of oil continuously.

After a few minutes, when you have finished pouring all the oil, the mayonnaise will be ready, with the right consistency, soft and light.

This type of mayonnaise also has the prerogative to keep in the fridge, put in a glass jar, even for ten days.

Shortcrust pastry

Ingredients for 8 people

Flour 12 oz - butter 2 oz - margarine or lard 2 oz - sugar 5 oz - 3 egg yolks - 1 drop of milk - grated ½ lemon - salt

PREPARATION

Prepare the shortcrust pastry by placing the sprinkle flour, sliced butter, lard or margarine, sugar, egg yolks, a pinch of salt and a dash of milk on the table.

Knead quickly and you will see that soon the dough will come off your hands and the table. Put the dough together and put it in a cool and sheltered place, covered with a cloth to let it rest for at least two hours.

Shortcrust pastry is the basis of many recipes, some of which you will find in this recipe book.

TUNA IN OIL

Ingredients

Fresh tuna 80 oz - water 4 quart - salt 10 oz - the juice of 2 lemons and their skins - 1 onion - 1 sprig of laurel

PREPARATION

I recommend you prepare this type of tuna in oil because, if packaged with the right precautions, it will be a valuable reserve for the winter.

First of all, the fish must be very fresh and, to recognize that it is, it must have a beautiful appearance with firmly firm meat, the eye must be alive, bright and red gills.

Cut the fish into pieces after having washed it well, put it in a pan with a capacity of at least 6 liters (the liquid must not come out) with 4 quarts of water and all the ingredients; bring to a boil and allow the fish to cook over moderate heat for about 3 hours and then cool in its broth.

After a few hours, remove the touches of the tuna, dry them with a cloth and put them, covered with cloths above and below, on a sieve or on the grill of the oven so that they continue to dry for at least 24 hours. In order for the fish to dry properly, it must be placed in a ventilated and cool place.

Then you can put it in a 1 quart glass jar, gradually covering it with oil (half of olive and half of seeds), about 10 deciliters will be enough.

Leave the jar open again for 24 hours and in case add more oil, if the tuna had absorbed it during the rest.

Cover the top with laurel leaves and close the jar to savor it when you want.

9 781914 384190